LIGHTWEIGHT CAMPING

LIVING IN THE GREAT OUTDOORS

by John Traynor

CICERONE

2 POLICE SQUARE, MILNTHORPE, CUMBRIA, LA7 7PY
www.cicerone.co.uk

Printed by KHL Printing, Singapore

A catalogue record for this book is available from the British Library.

To Fran for her love, care and unswerving support.

ACKNOWLEDGEMENTS

Too many people have spent time putting up with and helping me over years of travelling and camping in so many countries to list them all here. However, I would like to thank the countless farmers and others, whose names I never knew, who unfailingly extended a warm welcome and useful advice. May the Great Spirit of Reciprocity guard you all. Website details of the suppliers who kindly helped by supplying information and/or images can be found in Appendix A. Thanks also to The Camping and Caravanning Club (see Introduction), John Muir Trust (www.jmt.org) and Adam Bage.

CONTENTS

PREFACE

Pinning down a precise definition of lightweight camping is rather like trying to bottle thin mist. Although usually associated with walking and cycling, paddling and motorbike touring are also in the frame, and much lightweight camping will be car-based. Then there's the context of climate, terrain, weather, altitude, budget, skills and experience; and, to confuse the issue even more, these days campers are encouraged to transfer an urban lifestyle into their outdoor leisure with tents kitted out with the bedrooms, fitted carpets, wardrobes and kitchen units spurned by lightweight campers.

It's easy to caricature the approach as simply snapping the end off a toothbrush and paring bristles. In reality, lightweight camping is a relative term – an activity based on fairly flexible criteria – so you won't find a series of absolutes between these covers unless, of course, I believe they're really needed.

Adventure comes in many forms, but it's hard to beat camping – whatever age you are – as a brilliant way of stripping away the complexities of life and enjoying your own thoughts or sharing time with others. Having spent so much of my life out and about with a tent (and even more time with camping trips on my mind) it's always been fun to share the experiences, skills, gear and opportunities.

This book reflects a personal journey of the discovery of how little you need with you to enjoy living – and thriving rather than just surviving – in the outdoors. It aims to share the spirit and shed some light on the freedom to be enjoyed, hopefully showering information and advice and some inspiration, whether you're new to the game or a seasoned lightweight camper.

John Traynor

INTRODUCTION

WHY LIGHTWEIGHT CAMP?

Away, away, from men and towns,
To the wild wood and the downs –
To the silent wilderness…

'The Invitation' Percy Bysshe Shelley

Flexibility – freedom – fun – key words that explain why lightweight camping is a great way of enjoying life outdoors. Throw in great value for money and it is unbeatable. Whether your tented camp is a springboard for active outdoor adventure or a base for leisurely pursuits, you're in control, free to come and go as you please in the fresh air. Within minutes of arriving at a campsite, your new home can be under construction with shelter, kitchen, dining and sleeping needs all taking shape, and a tasty brew on the go.

'Lightweight camping' is not an absolute term. It is often as much an attitude of mind as anything else; one person's essential item may be another's luxury option. Then there's the choice of transport: on foot, by bike, paddling and, of course, engine power. Happily, there is no hierarchy in lightweight camping. Less weight is not inherently better in

Forget crumbling country piles: pick a tent for flexible outdoor living

what is, by and large, a non-competitive recreational activity. Skills and experience are key elements in the mix, complementing the role of gear. There are no hard and fast rules – just personal preferences – and this book considers the many ways of being a lightweight camping fan.

It is certainly not a dark art, but it would be easy to think so if you roamed around internet forums for too long. After a while you could almost be forgiven for thinking you had stumbled onto a strange subculture. For some, lightweight camping is a means to an end; for others, it's the end itself. Wherever you stand on the spectrum, enjoy it.

A word is needed here about my definition of 'camping'. The term has been hijacked by all sorts, even caravanners. Likewise, the term 'backpacking' now has as much to do with budget mooching around southeast Asia as it does with self-propelled lightweight camping. In this book, 'camping' means using a tent or other easily portable shelter such as a tarp (tarpaulin). 'Lightweight' means shelter, sleeping and kitchen gear that one person can carry. From this baseline veering towards ultra-lightweight is fine, but there is no place for tipis, yurts, or multi-berth tents with wardrobes and kitchen units.

ENDLESS OPPORTUNITIES

A fascinating way of spending a few hours of leisure is to sit down with a paper and pencil and work out in minute detail the preparations for an expedition into unexplored country.

Blank on the Map
Eric Shipton, 1938

For many, lightweight camping enables the self-contained exploration of swathes of country, whether self-propelled or touring by car or motorbike, moving on each day. For others, a fixed base allows several options: daily expeditions, sitting back and enjoying the scenery from the tent, discovering the beach or countryside on the doorstep. It is this freedom – the combination of opportunities without restrictions – that becomes so addictive. Although the appeal of unknown country is seductive, activities don't have to be demanding. Camping is a great way to enjoy hobbies and interests around the country – photography, bird watching, air shows, car rallies, film and music festivals – whatever takes your fancy.

The big plus about doing it all with a tent is that these opportunities can be embraced with a minimum of fuss and planning. With camping gear to hand at home, spontaneity can be the norm. You can take advantage of sunny spells, enjoy unexpected free time to the full, and at short notice swap home routine for an exploration of new areas and activities. Many campers meet up with old friends or make new ones on their trips, all enjoying life in different environments.

Compared to jetting off to a hotel abroad, camping falls firmly into the 'green' category. It is also far cheaper, if you look on buying camping gear as an investment rather than a cost. As well as saving money in the short and long terms, the benefits are reaped as both happy memories and the old cliché 'quality time'. Your first camping trip might be a tad disorganised, but you will soon learn how to stow gear and get everything shipshape – and does it really matter anyway? Over time your problems will turn into anecdotes, disasters into epics, and frustrations to laughter.

There are various 'ages' of campers. When you're young, economy is often a driving force, necessitating a small tent and very basic gear. With a family comes an expansion of both in size and complexity. As empty nesters, the need for a bigger tent and loads of gear eases off and you can enjoy a return to younger days – until the grandchildren join you. Similarly, the type of site can change over time from wild camping through basic farm sites to destination sites complete with swimming pool, pub and pizzeria. With thousands of sites to choose from in the UK alone (as well as open country: see Chapter 6), you need never be stuck for an option.

Loading up a car allows campers more scope for comfort, but doesn't mean taking the proverbial kitchen sink. Even so, the real freedom comes when packing a car, rucksack, canoe or panniers with lightweight tent, sleeping bag and stove and heading off into the unknown. With everything you need to survive (and thrive) to hand, you can go as you please.

Planning the next day's adventure

11

As bushcraft and outdoor living expert Ray Mears succinctly put it, 'Knowledge combined with experience is far more important than equipment.' This guide aims to help you move some way along the lightweight camping skills spectrum (if not how to survive Mears-style in deserts, jungles or the Arctic). Imagination will then be the only limit on your camping experience. Time to let it loose...

A CENTURY OF LIGHTWEIGHT CAMPING

The origins of recreational lightweight camping are clear. Putting to one side the odd adventures of various literary figures and Victorian climbers, they can sensibly be identified as the responsibility of Thomas Hiram (known as 'TH') Holding, born in 1844.

Although a keen canoe-camper, he inspired the establishment of the Cyclists' Touring Club; publication of his book *Cycle and Camp in Connemara* in 1898 prompted the eventual setting up of the Association of Cycle Campers, forerunner of The Camping Club and, eventually, The Camping and Caravanning Club (www.camping andcaravanningclub.co.uk). Trained as a tailor, Holding's enquiring nature led him to develop and make lightweight camping gear, particularly tents (one of which, made from silk, weighed only a few ounces).

TH Holding as an early backpacker (The Camping and Caravanning Club archive)

Fascinating pictures of camping in the early 20th century can be found in *First in the Field*, written by Hazel Constance and published by the Club in 2001. Although it has changed a great deal over the years, The Camping and Caravanning Club still welcomes lightweight campers.

The 'Outdoor Classics' boxes throughout this guide contain extracts from other classic books about camping published over the past 100 years; full references are given in Appendix B.

Another from the archive – TH Holding (right) on a canoe-camping trip with his son (The Camping and Caravanning Club archive)

COAST TO COAST ON THE SAINTS' WAY

With only a weekend to spare and a fine weather forecast, our thoughts turned to a spring backpacking trip with a clearly defined beginning and end, preferably combined with a theme that would add an extra dimension to the scenery. Backpacking is not only about trekking through high mountains and crossing remote passes: it can be a relaxed and sociable activity. A coast-to-coast walk sounded ideal, but where – and how long would it take? The answer lay in England's southwest peninsula.

The Saints' Way (*Forth an Syns* in Cornish) crosses mid-Cornwall from Padstow on the north coast to the south coast port of Fowey, a distance of some 30 miles. It appeared to follow a varied course through valleys, woodlands, pastures, moors and villages. By travelling light, it formed an easy two-day backpacking jaunt combining scenery, history and plenty of opportunity to explore and relax, without any pressure to be somewhere at a particular time. Summer-weight sleeping bags, self-inflating mats, a lightweight tent, stove and cooking gear made up the basics. Being ruthless about weight and bulk meant it all fitted into modest-sized rucksacks enabling us to travel easily across the county.

Although there is no real historical evidence of the existence of a true 'Saints' Way', sections of the trail are known to be ancient routes connecting shrines, standing stones, holy wells, chapels and churches. Footpaths, bridleways, ancient tracks and country lanes have been linked together to form a fairly direct cross-county trail that may well have been used by Christian missionaries and pilgrims in the Dark and Middle Ages. It was also known as the Mariners' Way and used by traders from Ireland and Wales who wanted to avoid the treacherous waters around the Cornish coast. You don't get a route more clearly defined at start and finish than by the sea, so the Great Trans-Cornwall Expedition was born and soon underway.

At the northern end of the route, Padstow proved delightful and the walk proper started at the lychgate of the church dedicated to St Petroc, Cornwall's 'national' saint. We climbed out of Padstow and crossed small creeks along the Camel estuary before turning inland to Little Petherick, leaving the sea to head south – to the sea again. Ahead lay St Breock Downs with the blades of the wind farm's towers visible from afar. On the map, the longstone of Men Gurta or 'stone of waiting' seemed a good place to pause for refreshment, but the clue provided by the wind turbines escaped us until we found for ourselves that the howling wind made Men Gurta rather less than attractive as a stopping point.

With an attractive section of old tracks, prehistoric remains, ancient bridges, farmsteads and hamlets ahead, we ploughed on with the wind at our backs to Withiel. After a pause for tea and rolls, we struck out for Tremore, the semi-sunken Withielgoose Lane offering a real flavour of ancient ways.

By and large, the Way is well waymarked, though many painted signs are very weatherbeaten, and the route guide is clear. As ever, it paid to read ahead and to use the OS Landranger map as well (200, Newquay & Bodmin).

Shortly after Tremore lay Lanivet, the halfway point and our pre-arranged pitch in a field owned by a friend of a friend (one of the advantages of Facebook for light-weight camping). Plenty of fresh water from a field tap was a real bonus. Snug against a hedge, it took just minutes to set up home and get a meal underway. It was late when we arrived, having dawdled and been diverted by curiosity in the afternoon, but being self-contained meant we had no need to stick to a schedule or stock up at a shop. We woke early and got on the trail after a breakfast cuppa, halting a couple

Stepping out on ancient tracks

A sheltered pitch on a freshly mown field

of hours later for a proper breakfast. Afterwards, with only the makings of lunch left to eat, the packs were even lighter and we speeded up without realising it. In backpacking, the usual equation is 'Lighter weight = further and faster' (or, of course, as far as you like in your own time with no need to stick to a rigid plan).

An early start saw us high – relatively – on Helman Tor without a soul in sight. (Indeed, we saw no other walkers or backpackers on the route over our two-day jaunt.) A welcome breeze proved fleeting as we embarked on a longish section of ancient hedged drovers' track that sheltered us and raised the temperature several degrees. At Lanlivery we paused to air feet and slake thirsts with a quick brew, and it wasn't long before we were chatting to locals about the village and the Way. Time slipped by, but with many miles to go we avoided the pub and upped the pace away from this attractive, lively village.

The busy A390 came as a shock after our quiet meanderings, but after a few hundred metres we turned off and turned back the clock again as we descended a heavily rutted bridleway, at times more like a streambed. We thought we had made a route-finding error, but soon emerged near Milltown. As with many places along the route, this 'village' proved to be a handful of cottages and a house that was once, long ago, a pub.

From here we followed the River Fowey down to journey's end but, as is often the case, the final miles seemed interminable. Glimpses of the river and the picturesque church of St Winnow on the far bank kept our spirits high as we sped along before dropping down to cheery Golant before following a path across the Downs with wonderful views of the estuary.

A final section along the busy road was marred slightly by drivers who appeared to think that grazing backpackers with the wings of their cars was acceptable behaviour (another use for trekking poles was discovered as we swung them about with gay abandon and avoided injury). As it marks the 'official' end of the Way, we brushed our fingers along the wall of the church of St Fimbarrus for form's sake. A welcome beer hit the spot while we waited for a taxi back to Padstow and the car.

TENT LIFE

By the time that dusk came creeping up the heather-covered moorland, all three tents were up, the groundsheets were put down, and the sleeping-bags unrolled on them.

Five Go Off To Camp Enid Blyton, 1945

The most important thing about a tent is to pitch it properly.

Camp and Trek
Jack Cox, 1956

Regardless of what tent you use, where you are and how you are travelling, Jack Cox's advice is universal. There are no hard and fast rules about camping, which is one reason why you will not find definitive checklists in this book. That's not to say that making up your own won't be a great help in never forgetting the (now mostly redundant) tin opener. Flexibility characterises all aspects, and it's partly that openness that makes it so attractive.

On a National Park campsite in South Africa I once helped an elderly couple lift their fridge freezer from the back of their pick-up and manoeuvre it under a huge awning. About the only thing they lacked on the pitch was a plumbed-in washing machine. 'Lacked', that is, if you want to recreate home under canvas. They did as they were staying for four months, having retired from the National Park

Service after over 40 years, and still entitled to camp for free: theirs was the Rolls Royce of basecamps.

My disbelief was softened later by an ice-cold beer plucked from that fridge. We talked about their experiences backpacking – safaris, bush camps, canoe camping – and a wide range of outdoor topics. They had a rich vein of knowledge about camping and I mined it happily for several hours. 'Horses for courses' summed up the old boy's camping philosophy, and it struck a chord.

THE UNOFFICIAL RULES OF CAMPING

- Lightweight gear gets heavier by the hour when carried in a rucksack.
- Nothing is unbreakable.
- Guylines roam around in the dark.
- Tent problems only develop in the rain.
- Airbeds only collapse when you're asleep.
- Sleeping bag zips always jam when you need a pee – desperately.
- Stove gas usually runs out ten minutes before the food is cooked.
- Bottle openers are camouflage experts.
- 'Sleeps four' means 'Sleeps two normal-sized adults'.
- Emergencies never happen at a convenient time and place.
- Good humour is contagious.

1 BASECAMP

Basecamps are not reserved for Himalayan expeditions. Camping as a base for walking and climbing pre-dates backpacking and remains the norm for tens of thousands of outdoor enthusiasts each year. Pitching on a commercial site offers a range of facilities and avoids the gradual pollution of the environment through wild camping sanitation – no matter how well good practice is carried out (see Chapter 6).

THE RIGHT TENT FOR THE JOB

Funnily enough, it was a tent called the Himalayan Hotel that served as the base for an ambitious plan to paddle all the open water in the Lake District. We knew we would be tired each day so picked a campsite next to Ullswater with basic but sound facilities, and within walking distance of a pub with great bar meals. Not expedition fare, admittedly, but this was supposed to be a holiday. As it turned out, a tent designed for high mountain use proved to be a treasure. After a day battling gale-force winds on Ullswater the canoe had to be lashed to a handy tree to stop it blowing away, and the value of a roomy tent was driven home as the next two days were spent eating, sleeping and reading inside. Other people packed up and fled for home as the weather got worse. It was a useful reminder that foul weather can be encountered anywhere (and although ours qualified as a basecamp, the idea that it was the type where we would lounge around on chairs sipping aperitifs before dinner was hilarious). The only chair that came our way bounced off the tent on its way to the lake as gusts of wind hit scary heights.

Camping on Skye – a great base for
most outdoor pursuits

Most basecamps are uneventful, with a fair degree of extra comfort than that usually enjoyed when on the move. Staying in one place for a few days means it is worth beefing up lighting, seating, food preparation, cooking and eating (and, of course, camping is not all about outdoor activities: camping near Kendal for the Mountain Festival one year was about convenience, cost, preference and spending time with friends).

These days you can buy wardrobes, storage and kitchen units for camping trips but that scene is far removed from lightweight. If planning to spend a few nights on the same site, do some research to pick somewhere suitable that has the right facilities for your party. Fortunately, there is a wide spectrum of campsite styles with enough options to suit all campers' needs. Don't make assumptions about character, facilities, prices, size, rules, restrictions, allocation and distribution of pitches but check before booking. Prices can vary substantially and are sometimes counterintuitive – a site with a few basic facilities may well be more expensive than a super-equipped site but have great views. You'll soon learn how to interpret descriptions and start forming your own list of favourite spots.

Directories and website forums can be useful (see Appendix A) but nothing beats word of mouth. Picking where to pitch on site needs careful consideration as well.

Directories and website forums are useful sources for site selection but nothing beats word of mouth

On farm sites you may be spoiled for choice when it comes to picking a pitch

PICKING A PITCH

What makes a pitch perfect varies so much, depending on individual requirements, that you're unlikely to come across a queue for a specific spot. Your pitch could range from a vast expanse of grassy bank by a river on a simple farm site to a marked-out pitch on a large commercial site complete with water and electricity supply. Obviously, the cost per night will vary depending on the services offered.

Cosy? Or too close for comfort?

Not so obvious is a varying level of charges on many commercial sites depending on the size of pitch. Apart from the basic consideration of pitch size, shape and services, the major hidden factor in pitch selection is surface. As a camper, you might assume it would be grass, but as the ground on popular sites takes quite a hammering, marked-out pitches may be 'seeded' with gravel to make a firmer surface (not good for groundsheets).

Being near to or far from loos and showers depends on a host of personal considerations as well your tolerance of streams of foot traffic. A pitch on main thoroughfares to these amenities is likely to suffer lights burning all night; pack eyeshades and earplugs. Easier to decide on are rubbish bins and water supply taps. Avoiding proximity to the former is obvious; if you like the regular drumming of water into plastic containers and the shrieks of those filling them, then a pitch next to taps will not be a problem.

Location, location, location: a mantra that the media has been hurling at us for years. It is easy to understand its importance if your pitch is near a site shop, pizzeria, beer garden, play area or swimming pool. The pluses and minuses of convenience, noise and people traffic need to be weighed up. Avoiding being near the site entrance and reception is a 'no brainer': does anyone really enjoy listening to loud car radios and slamming doors whilst choking on exhaust fumes? Such factors confirm why there is a natural affinity between lightweight campers and farm sites. If your basecamp is off-site on a 'wild' pitch then a key consideration is sanitation (see Chapter 6).

When you find a site you love and plan to come back, make a note of which pitch suits you best and request it on booking. Take a picture to help stake your claim. As your choice of pitch may be restricted on site, it pays to pack a variety of pegs to ensure your tent is secure whether the ground is hard or soft. Traditional advice suggests you pitch your tent with the doorway facing the rising sun. Putting to one side the much more flexible tent designs on offer these days, it is a priority to minimise the effect of the wind. If you can, pitch your tent with the main door/s facing away from the prevailing wind.

Level grass, open aspect and glorious sunshine at The Willows campsite on the Lleyn Peninsula in Wales (www.abersochcampsites.co.uk)

- **Size** Is it big enough and the right shape? Being cheek-by-jowl with neighbours is hardly a great way to spend nights in a tent. If pitches are designed for large family tents, you'll be camping in the middle of carts, kids and chaos. Check out the pitches before booking in.

- **Location** How far are the loos and showers? Being far away is usually preferable to pitching next door and enduring the noise.

- **People traffic** If you're on a through route to amenities, you'll soon get fed up with inane queries such as, 'Can you really be comfortable in that little tent?' and the like.

- **Style** Most large sites have pitches marked out and numbered. Where you can pick your own unmarked pitch you may discover a universal occasional rule of camping. If you camp in a quiet corner of a large empty field, somebody will choose to pitch right next to you.

- **Trees** Apart from the doom-laden warnings about falling branches and lightning strikes, think about whether or not you want to pitch your tent in the shade.

- **Facilities** Most of us just want clean water plus toilets and washrooms, and almost all commercial sites will offer these. Having had to sweep out and clean some facilities before using them, don't assume that a nice sign and a fee guarantees cleanliness.

- **Pitch** Key considerations include surface, slope and the windbreak of a hedge.

- **Rubbish bins** Camping near these is usually a bad move even if they are well-maintained rather than rubbish-strewn – think about smell, insect life and vermin.

- **View** Open countryside is ideal, but you might end up staring at neighbours or site facilities.

1

BASECAMP

ON-SITE ETIQUETTE

Tent living is supposed to be simple and uncomplicated; following campsite rules and advice helps make it so for everybody. Despite the appeal of 'getting away from it all', at peak times even simple farm campsites can be pretty busy with campers and caravanners living in close proximity and sharing all the facilities. There's more to staying on a campsite than just rolling up and pitching in, but most 'site etiquette' comes down to a combination of common sense, courtesy and mutual respect.

Written rules on sites are usually prominent and easy to follow; the unwritten rules tend to be based on mutual consideration. As far as making sense of the rules and customs goes, the simple advice is be aware and ask if in doubt. That's harder if you're camping abroad and don't know the language, but perseverance and good humour usually win the day – as will a quick apology if you've inadvertently upset somebody.

If there is a motto for good site etiquette then it is, undoubtedly, 'Do unto your campsite and fellow campers as you would have them do unto you.'

It sounds obvious but if the rules note 'don't do it' about something specific, then don't do it. Some are obvious, such as speed limits, vehicle access hours and pets on leads, especially on farms; others less so. Rather than ignoring those rules you cannot see a reason for, ask for an explanation.

Keeping your pitch clean and free from rubbish benefits everybody, and there is no excuse for litter around a tent. Apart from looking scruffy, it might attract vermin and is inconsiderate to your neighbours (who might be a lot closer than those at home). Dump rubbish after every meal and fall into line with the site's recycling policy – it's simply a matter of respect.

Most campsites expect noise be kept to a minimum after a certain time, usually around 10pm. It's not only loud music that needs to be considered but also loud voices, laughter and arguments, as well as car door slamming. On an otherwise quiet site, any noise is hugely amplified. If your neighbours complain, you might be asked to leave.

Respecting the privacy of others is important anywhere, so cutting through other people's pitches to save a few yards' walk isn't on, even when it's raining. Staring at people eating a meal is just plain rude (even if you're fascinated by the aroma and what the food might be).

Parents of small children should make sure they know where they are and what they're up to. Being responsible includes not expecting neighbours to keep an eye on them or allowing them to embark on irritating antics such as tripping over guylines or crashing bikes into tents. If you are camping without children (and would prefer to remain that way) there are commercial sites that only accept adults (www.ukcampsite.co.uk).

Most people take a camera on holiday, but respect the privacy of others when snapping away on site and be sensitive to their wish not to be photographed.

Keeping your eyes and ears open in strange environments will help you make the most of your holiday. Being a thoughtful and considerate camper helps to make your stay – and that of those around you – relaxing and enjoyable.

DOGS ON SITE

Although I'm not anti-dog, I believe dogs should be banned from campsites. I am fed up with inconsiderate dog owners met both on country walks and on campsites. It's bad enough encountering a barking bounding dog off its lead on a walk: when the dog 'nips' an ankle the owner comments, 'Honestly, he's never done that before.' An unreserved apology is unusual. It beggars belief that owners can watch their dogs urinate on tents without stopping them. I once had an owner comment that his dog was 'Just marking his territory.' Wrong: my tent is my territory. Despite signs on sites concerning the need to keep dogs on leads, some people blithely ignore them – and I've watched dogs foul play areas whilst their selfish owners studiously look the other way.

However, wanting to take your dog on holiday with you is understandable, but consider the following:

- Check that dogs are allowed on any sites you have in mind.
- Ideally, pick a site where pets are catered for and positively welcomed.
- If pets are allowed, check about any extra charges and specific rules.
- Only take a well-behaved pet; dogs that love to bark at strangers – canine or human – will irritate people.
- Keep your dog on a short lead at all times, both on and off site (it's easy to think that on open moorland without a soul about your dog can run free: but be aware of the damaging disturbance to nesting birds).
- Clear up any mess your dog leaves and dispose of it properly.
- Don't leave your dog locked in your car; if sleeping in the tent with you is not an option, have a dog-free holiday.
- Don't tie your dog to trees or bushes.
- Make sure your dog doesn't scare local wildlife or farm animals.
- Even when right off the beaten track, keep to urban 'poop and scoop' practice. It's more than depressing to tread in dog faeces on a narrow mountain trail.

OUTDOOR CLASSICS

In a collection of essays, the American novelist and environmentalist Wallace Stegner noted factors that made a wild spot ideal for camp.

This place has everything – every essential, every conceivable extra. It has the level ground, the good grass, the wood, the easy access to water, that make a camp comfortable. It has the shelter and shade, the wide views, the openness and breeziness that raise comfort to luxuriousness. There are no mosquitoes on that clifftop; there are trees shaped to the back where a man can sit and read; the ground is the coarse granular kind that produces no dust and that, in the remote possibility of rain, would not produce mud either.

Where the Bluebird Sings to the Lemonade Springs Wallace Stegner, 1992

2 ON THE MOVE

Many and varied are the ways and means of travelling the country with camping gear to hand. However, whether wild or on site, under your own steam or by motor, there are core means of transport that are usually considered the norm: so apologies to those who pedal tricycles, sail open boats, fly micro-lights or drive traction engines to get around. I've come across campers using them all, but you won't find them in this book. One of the most inspiring was a chap in his 80s who I met in Torridon. Having walked and camped for most of his life, his knees could no longer take the strain of ruck-sack and hill paths. Instead, he had made a small trolley and wandered the quiet roads of the Highlands towing his camping gear behind him. From spring to autumn he meandered along, making new friends every year and making the most of what he could do, rather than complaining about what he couldn't. I'm sure his spirit roams the Highlands yet.

The modern car and the modern light-weight camping outfit make such a perfect combination that it is not surprising to find experts estimating that motorists make up eighty per cent of the campers today.

Camping
R McCarthy, 1947

Smaller lightweight tents are ideal for touring by car – quick to pitch and taking up little space when packed away

Thirlspot Farm Camping is a simple farm site in the Lake District, handy for walkers tackling Helvellyn (very handy, in fact, as a track to the summit starts from the back of the farmyard). It attracts a wide variety of campers, most arriving by car and preferring to camp with fairly basic kit: a practical windbreak, a couple of light folding chairs and a small table being the usual concessions to comfort.

With shared interests there's often an easy-going camaraderie on such sites, without infringing on the privacy of others. 'Nice tent' here usually means a lightweight model that takes up little space at home, in the car and on site. A group of us had gathered clutching mugs of tea to discuss whether the large bird seen that day was really a golden eagle, or just wishful thinking. As a large people carrier pulled up nearby, the chat fell away as it became apparent that it held a couple and a lot of gear. We watched as a couple of tent bags, table, big chairs and assorted bags and boxes appeared and were carefully laid out.

As we dispersed to our pitches, the couple started erecting the tent. An hour or so later, a tent big enough to house a family of eight or more, complete with bedrooms, several doorways and a massive awning had been built. The big table was set up in what was obviously the dining area, not far from a camp kitchen unit that looked quite complex from afar.

They spent even more time putting together a wardrobe and smaller storage units before starting to pump up what turned out to be the mother of all airbeds. They to have every available item of camping kit. Engaging them in conversation, I asked them how long they were stopping. 'Just the one night,' came the cheery reply. It had taken them about two hours to set up their tent and paraphernalia, but they seemed happy. A neighbour noted, 'Somebody should tell them it's not about the gear.' Another added, shaking his head, 'They wouldn't listen.'

A tad unfair, perhaps, but the lighter the weight the more time there is for fun. In the morning we were all on our way while the heavyweights were deconstructing their temporary home. Each to their own.

BY CAR

Car camping isn't about driving all day taking in the scenery through the windscreen. Instead, the changes in location can involve walks, other activities and visits to attractions. Just because the car can carry the load easily doesn't mean it should be packed out with gear 'just in case'.

Nobody in their right minds wants to spend hours pitching a tent, sorting the camp and getting organised only to take it all apart in the morning, move on and repeat the process somewhere else. You need a tent that can be whipped up and down quickly and easily. A porch of sorts is useful for cooking and eating, and a windbreak offers extra privacy as well as fulfilling its main role. You might want to reconsider usual practice and eat out in cafés and pubs, thus only needing a small stove for brews and basic 'kitchen' gear for sandwiches and snacks. It takes a different mind-set to enjoy a busy day, find a site, pitch your

Do not take any more than is absolutely necessary.

Gilcraft's column, *The Scout* magazine, 12 May 1928

tent, have a shower and head off out again, but it is hardly revolutionary or demanding.

Packing
Tough boxes are great for camping hardware such as cooking and eating gear, preferably packed in the boot with table, chairs, airbeds and tent, whilst soft luggage is fine for clothes. Sleeping bags make great comfort cushions for passengers, but aim not to have seats and floor space jammed with stuff. As well as being uncomfortable, it is potentially dangerous.

As cars get smaller, not all the camping gear will fit in the boot. Lining roof storage boxes with plenty of waterproof material allows the contents to be well wrapped up and protected if it rains. Soft systems take up little space stored at home, and soft luggage is easier to pack and handle.

Roof-top tents
Popular for expeditions, on safari and in some European countries, these are rarely seen on campsites. They offer a safe night's sleep a few feet above the ground, but you need to be something of a gymnast to get in and out via a ladder.

On the road
Forward planning loads the dice in favour of fun rather than foul days. Sort out the route finding, keep all your important papers together, safe and handy, and make sure everybody is comfortable. Everyone has their own ways of making the most of car journeys, but here a few tried and tested ways to enjoy the trip:

Roof storage options extend a car's carrying capacity without compromising comfort and safety inside

- Allow ample time rather than set an unrealistic or demanding schedule: take into account whether you have to travel at a peak holiday time and adjust plans and expectations accordingly
- Allow ample time rather than set an unrealistic or demanding schedule, and take the stress out of in-car route finding with satellite navigation. Bearing in mind the limitations of sat nav systems, an OS map, a compass and the ability to use them cannot be underestimated!
- Have plenty of favourite music – plug in the iPod or make up your own 'car mix' compilation CDs.
- Talking books seem to eat up journey times.
- Regular breaks ease in-car tensions and help to keep drivers alert.
- When you pitch up on site, make a fresh brew and unwind before making camp.
- Pack a coolbox and flasks with food and drink for the route; being self-contained saves time, money and aggravation.
- Instead of a bulky washbag, use a lightweight travellers' washkit. These take up little space and are far handier to carry, hang up and use when you head off to the shower block.
- The easiest way to keep track of key paperwork, tickets, credit cards and money on holiday is to use a neat document wallet. Keeping it all together focuses the mind on not losing it.
- When you need some form of breakdown assistance, you really need it. That annual charge always seems like a bargain if you give it a miss and the car then breaks down on holiday.
- If travelling with children you'll know, presumably, all about their likes, dislikes and travel foibles. It pays to keep wet wipes handy for spills.
- Adults and children alike benefit from regular stops to relieve boredom, stiffness and bladders.

Legal and safe

Be prepared for roadside car problems by carrying an emergency pack. You can avoid the expense of a prepacked kit by pulling together your own. Winter driving advice makes hitting the road sound like an Arctic expedition; that for driving abroad stresses fines and hassles for not carrying a variety of items. It's sensible to carry those on the following list and to learn (in advance) how to change a light bulb or fuse. This is really basic – more than emergency – kit.

Remember that every item used for camping has to be packed, unpacked and repacked again for each trip, therefore be ruthless and weed out every unnecessary item. And remember, also, that every ounce has to be moved by expensive petrol.

Caravanning & Camping for Motorists John Yoxall, 1957

- **Warning triangle** Sturdy enough not to blow over when heavy wagons roar past; a weighted sock helps.
- **Bright fluorescent reflective vest** Makes excellent sense, especially when changing an offside tyre at the roadside.
- **Fire extinguisher** Every home/car/tent should have one.
- **Spare fuses** Sometimes simply changing a blown fuse can have you on your way in minutes.
- **Spare light bulbs** Another easy way to sort a potential problem.
- **First aid kit** Make it fairly comprehensive, resisting the tropical medicine and covering the everyday problems.
- **Jump leads** Useful when the coolbox is left plugged in and drains the battery.
- **Torch** Having one with a long lead that draws power from a car accessory socket means there is no need to worry about dead batteries when you need a really good light source.
- **Basic tools**

ON FOOT

Backpacking has always been with us; it used to be known simply as 'walking and camping'. Derrick Booth's classic Backpacker's Handbook got the UK scene underway in the early 1970s, and the notion – and associated gear – has since developed apace.

Much has been made in recent years of the lightweight revolution in backpacking gear. The focus has been on shaving grams and ounces rather than on honing skills and attitudes. For some, backpacking is an art; for others, it is a science. For most, it's a great way to experience life outdoors, and is best described as 'magic'.

Gear and skills are involved, of course, but they are means to an end: walking through a landscape carrying everything needed for a comfortable night or more outdoors on one's back in a rucksack, without the need to be anywhere at a particular time. It's not a survival challenge, or escapism, but it's all about getting in touch with reality – and certainly not to be confused with the budget travellers mooching around the world on gap years, who hijacked the word.

The simple pleasure of waking on a mountain summit, clifftop or riverbank after a sound night in a cosy sleeping bag shouldn't be underestimated. Stripped of all life's usual distractions, it becomes much easier to think clearly (or, indeed, not

Afoot and light-hearted
  I take to the open road,
Healthy, free, the world
  before me,
The long brown path before
  me leading wherever I
  choose…

Song of the Open Road
Walt Whitman, 1900

Getting to and enjoying wild
places can be part of the
attraction of backpacking

think at all). Moving through the countryside with a flexible
schedule allows you to follow impulses, explore on a whim
and just have fun. How else can you have a succession of
'little places in the country' and spend so little on them?
A backpacking tent is truly the most cost-effective holiday
home.

Competition is not part of the backpacking scene. No
hierarchy of endeavour is involved, just the rewards gained
doing something you enjoy, be it a long-distance trail or a
couple of hours' walk in an evening to a great pitch. That
pitch doesn't have to be high, remote or otherwise difficult
to reach; and backpacking doesn't have to be long distance.
Don't let dreams of crossing Europe on foot stop you from
enjoying a local weekend's backpacking. Obvious factors
in choosing where to backpack include budget, the holiday
time available and season. Throw in style and the situation
becomes more interesting. If you're looking for solitude in
wild places, then the Ridgeway will not suit you. If your
style is ultra-light with frequent re-supply, then crossing
Iceland is a non-starter.

Having backpacked in Canada, the US, Iceland,
Scandinavia, Germany, Austria, France, Spain, Italy, Slovenia,

William Kemsley Jr, founder
of the American magazine
Backpacker, stated that
'Backpacking is not life-
changing but life-charging.
What you take away often
bears little relation to the effort
or time expended.' Spot on.

Turkey, Morocco and South Africa as well as throughout the UK, I find picking a favourite destination difficult. Each has its unique appeal, often influenced by my mood at the time, and that destination's challenges. Water was the main problem in both Iceland and Turkey – too much in the former, not enough in the latter.

One of my favourite backpacking areas is Cumbria and the Scottish Borders, where high and lonely places can be found alongside bustling valleys. Re-supply is easy, the scenery is magnificent, and the odd bar meal and pint always go down a treat. At times I relish meeting new people, at others I would rather be on my own: having options is the key. I didn't go to Nepal until I could spend several months there; others are happy with three weeks. There are no rules.

When backpacking bear in mind local customs, traditions and ways of dealing with environmental impact. Rather than use a tent on the Appalachian Trail, I 'camped' in open wooden shelters that eased the pressure of long-distance backpackers on the landscape. It's easy to have strong mixed feelings about such initiatives (and about such issues as paved sections of the Pennine Way). It is far harder, of course, to come up with a solution that protects the interests of both land and users.

As there is no right to camp where we like in most of the UK, leaving overnight pitches to chance is not recommended. Happily, wild camping is possible on Dartmoor (www.dartmoor-npa.gov.uk: search for 'wild camping') and Kielder Water, albeit with restrictions. Keilder Water's

ON THE MOVE

So much for 'wild' camping

backpacking sites take some finding (check in person at the information centre) – and that's the way it should be. Accommodation guides (including campsites) are published for many long-distance footpaths (LDPs), especially National Trails. The Backpackers Club's *LDP Site and Pitch Directory* is the only one of its type. Covering most of the established long-distance routes in the UK, it's compiled and updated by members and complements its *UK Farm Pitch Directory*. The Long Distance Walkers Association (LDWA: www.ldwa.org.uk) is another national club worth considering. Apart from their websites and publications, such clubs offer a rich network of knowledge and experience. Tourist boards, National Park information centres and commercial guides will also provide information. Pulling together a number of sites in a new area from a variety of sources and working out your own routes between several can while away many happy hours. Don't overlook scouring your map for likely pitches, and stop a little earlier than planned if a cracking site crops up.

Potential sites are not the only places to bear in mind when sorting out a route. Longer trips mean that the *poste restante* service at post offices is a useful resource for re-supply; it pays to check opening times for those in remote locations and small villages, and whether the post office marked on the OS map still exists: the national network has been much reduced recently. Pubs and hostels that offer camping are another potentially useful address for picking up parcels along your route – if you are stopping there, of course.

Plan and pitch
In magazines there is often an assumption that all backpacking trips are wilderness expeditions, involving danger and threats to survival. This assumption is usually linked to that of high mountaintops being the goal for all 'serious' backpackers, but in my experience backpacking along canal towpaths and coastal trails is as enjoyable as slogging up hillsides.

Backpacking is certainly not all about assessing risks in high mountains and expeditions to the wildest places. Sometimes it is great to walk with friends; sometimes solitude is welcome. Let somebody know where you are going and for how long and amble off on your own if the fancy takes you.

A journey of a thousand miles may well begin with just one step, but a successful backpacking jaunt needs a little more forethought; even the most relaxed backpacking vagabond must have, at least, a start point and initial direction. Sensibly, you should be planning where to go, how long it might take and where to pitch your tent safely, legally and with regard to the outdoor environment. Plus, of course, whether you are tracing the course of a river or following high mountain ridges, it makes sense to leave details of your proposed route and alternatives with family or friends. Routes and pitches are intertwined when you are planning – something of a chicken-and-egg scenario – so gather as much information as you can before spreading out the maps.

There is a tendency to overestimate the distances that can be achieved day after day, especially if longer backpacking jaunts are infrequent. Bearing in mind that backpacking is about leisure and recreation, try to be realistic when working out daily mileage, overnight stops and re-supply. Arriving in a village after its little shop has closed is likely to be inconvenient rather than a disaster, but could be avoided with realistic planning.

THE BACKPACKERS CLUB

The Backpackers Club (see Appendix A) is intended for those folk who enjoy lightweight self-contained camping whether walking, cycling, canoeing or cross-country skiing and has been called, wryly, 'the club for unclubbables' despite its truly friendly character. Founded in 1972, benefits to members have grown steadily with many services still unique to the club, including access to a comprehensive advice and information service on all aspects of backpacking and a quarterly magazine, postal library, backpacking weekends, *UK Farm Pitch Directory*, *LDP Site and Pitch Directory* and a list of companies offering discounts to members.

Rucksacks

Backpacking is as much an attitude of mind as anything else: you have the freedom to do as you please and, by and large, go where you like. How much weight you should carry on a backpacking trip is impossible to pin down: there are too many variables to consider, not least personal preference. How much you want to take and thus how much space is needed and the amount of weight involved will influence your choice of rucksack. When I look at my favourite rucksack of some 15 years ago it seems like a dinosaur (and weighs in like one as well).

Be realistic about your experience and aims when chatting to staff in a specialist outdoor shop, and take their advice on fit. As most shops tend to specialise in two or three rucksack brands, comparing a variety of back systems between a number of shops is often easier. For such a range of options, buying a rucksack in a popular outdoor recreation area such as the Lake District can be a plus (even though I usually favour supporting local shops). Good shops will have a range of soft weights available to simulate a loaded rucksack; don't buy one if you've only tried and adjusted it empty.

A holiday, and alone!
On foot, of course, for he must travel light. He would buckle on a pack after the approved fashion. That and a waterproof and a stick, and his outfit was complete.

Huntingtower
John Buchan, 1922

Solo or with friends – the decision is yours, but if you're splitting gear for carrying you can use a smaller capacity rucksack

The arrival of rucksacks with welded seams should have meant the end of waterproofing problems. No chance! You still have to open a rucksack to access the contents, and who's to say it won't end up in a stream or lake? It is always best to play safe: use a waterproof rucksack liner and rain cover, and pack your sleeping bag in plastic or a dry bag.

If money is no object you can save masses of weight on gear, including your rucksack. Most of us have to balance aspirations with budgets. Don't delay in heading off out because you haven't got the latest and lightest rucksack design.

Comfort and construction

Rucksack harness or suspension systems vary in detail and materials but all share the goals of ensuring comfort and easy adjustment, regardless of clever marketing descriptions. Shoulder straps and hip belts work in harness to share the load between chest and hips with the aid of a light flexible internal frame.

Ingenious foam and mesh back panels try to reduce sweaty back syndrome, but it's a fact of backpacking life for most of us. Shoulder straps, often contoured to follow a natural line, should be strong enough to hold their shape without chafing, pinching or sliding about; a linking chest strap ensures they stay in place. On backpacking rucksacks the hip belt is the main load-bearing component and usually has generous firm padding often moulded into a pre-formed shape that helps to hold the rucksack securely and comfortably on the hips.

Whether the rucksack you're considering comes in different sizes or has back length adjustment, getting the fit right is essential for comfort. Take the time and advice to get it right.

Quick and easy back length adjustment; but do you need it?

Rucksacks can take quite a hammering and should be designed to take it in their stride, so take a look at the detail before buying. Durability is a key consideration with materials, especially in areas of high wear which may benefit from reinforcement. Tightly stitched seams reduce the possibility of materials tearing or stitching coming apart; bar tacking at stress points such as shoulder straps is essential. The inside of seams should be bound to reduce abrasion and the easy ingress of water.

Check that all zips work smoothly and are stitched in securely. Likewise buckles – make sure they are sewn on the right way (this may sound obvious, but mistakes do happen).

Rucksacks for women
Women no longer have to endure poorly fitting rucksacks; most manufacturers now design and make harness systems specifically for them, including the following features:

- Hip belts sized and pre-curved to reflect differences in shape

There is no longer any need for women to endure poorly fitting, uncomfortable rucksacks

- Shoulder straps positioned closer together at the neck and shaped to cut away from the chest
- Back length width and adjustment
- Main pack compartment shape and size reflecting the dimensions of the harness.

THE RIGHT RUCKSACK FOR THE JOB

For many years I relished carrying a rucksack that was attached to an aluminium frame and featured pockets galore. Each pocket played its part in holding all the goodies I deemed necessary for backpacking, and I spent hours planning what to pack and how to pack it.

Then came internal framed rucksacks with only a couple of side pockets and a top pocket. Initially quite simple, these soon became more complex and their overall weight grew inexorably. In an attempt to control this weight increase I chose a model without pockets. With increased experience I realised that I didn't need all those gadgets, and that other developments – particularly in clothing – reinforced the point that the weight I needed to carry for comfort and safety had dropped substantially.

These days I favour simple rucksacks for most trips. As these usually span overnights and weekends, the total packed weight is relatively low (despite my keen interest in food).

For longer jaunts I favour more substantial back systems, trading the extra weight for more comfort with a heavier load. Regardless of how back systems for rucksacks are developed, basic principles endure – such as keep the load close to your back – and certain realities cannot be avoided – sweaty backs – whatever the manufacturers' claims.

It's a question of working out what suits you best, depending on what sort of trip you are planning. There are no hard and fast rules – just one of the joys of backpacking.

Packing it in

Some advice on packing a rucksack can be confusing. If heavy items should be carried low down, why do rucksacks have zipped bottom compartments promoted as ideal for sleeping bags? Sifting through (often contradictory) advice on load carrying and stability, I have reached the conclusion that much of it – coming from companies involved in climbing and skiing, for example – is irrelevant.

Obviously, a stable load is easier and safer to carry, but if you are wandering happily along a riverside footpath you don't need to worry greatly about load instability hurling you over a precipice. You won't always pack your rucksack to its full capacity, which is when load compression straps reduce the available volume and stop the load wobbling around.

The key elements to consider in packing are keeping some items really handy – such as waterproofs and first aid kit in the lid pocket – and others in the rough order you'll need them when pitching. As you'll want to get your tent staked out sharpish, packing it underneath everything else doesn't make sense. Keep the first items to be used handiest.

On the trail

When slogging up a hillside in hot sun your collection of lightweight gear will probably feel that it weighs a ton, and sometimes the anticipated view from the top isn't enough to keep those feet moving smoothly. Try breaking down the distance, counting your steps in the style of a mantra. Fifty is a good number; enough to feel you've made some progress when you pause for yet another breather.

Reading glasses need to be kept handy and well protected. A reinforced zipped case fastened securely to your hip belt keeps them safe and easy to access, such as when you suspect a navigation error.

A camera buried deep in your rucksack tends not to be used – it's usually too much hassle to retrieve it – so keep yours to hand in a lightly padded belt pouch

Sort out the cat's cradle of webbing straps that decorate many rucksacks by trimming off excess lengths and losing redundant straps completely. Seal the cut ends with a quick blast of flame and add your own accessory straps to suit.

It makes sense to keep items such as waterproofs and a first aid kit in your rucksack's top pocket where they are easy to find and quick to pull out when needed.

You lose quite a lot of fluid through sweating and that has to be replaced to maintain health and fitness. On the move, you could slip a hydration bladder (basically, a bag of water) into your rucksack and draw on the water supply via a flexible tube and bite valve as you walk. They are popular but, having had two big brand name bladders burst on me, I prefer the reliability of water bottles and take plenty of fluid on board before getting parched.

Mini karabiners are handy for clipping on all sorts of items, but should never be used as a climbing aid.

OUTDOOR CLASSIC

For his 3000-mile walk through Europe from Portugal to Italy, John Waite knew he had to rely on camping to keep within a tight budget.

My camping equipment included an 'A' frame, stormproof, rainproof tent with a flysheet, inner tent, aluminium poles and pegs. I had bought a Karrimat to sleep on, which would keep away the ground chill, and a good quality Black's Icelandic mummy sleeping bag that would keep me warm enough even if the temperature dropped below freezing. I was also carrying a sheet of polythene to go under the tent to protect its somewhat delicate-looking groundsheet.

As I refused to live on a diet of cold food and the budget did not stretch to more than the occasional meal in a restaurant, cooking equipment was an absolute necessity. The 'kitchen' consisted of an Optimus petrol stove with light aluminium pans and burner paste for starting the thing off, a petrol bottle (one litre), a water bottle, (one and a half litres), mess tins, tin opener, sponge and scourer, rag, knife, fork and spoon, a tin mug and matches carefully wrapped in a plastic bag so that they would not get damp.

In addition to this, in various pockets, were needle and thread, string, dubbin, glasses case with spare glasses, passport, cheque book, wallet, diary, address book, pen, book, compass, cigarettes and, most important, maps. The weight would be considerable since I had yet to include basic provisions, but it was a price I was prepared to pay for independence.

On foot, you can go where you want when you want, stopping at will and reaching places where no other form of transport will take you, not even the bicycle.

Mean Feat John Waite, 1985

One of the most-respected designer/manufacturers of outdoor gear is Pete Hutchinson of PHD Mountain Software. With many decades of hard-won experience behind him, he knows the score on quality lightweight gear. On the PHD website he notes:

Where 'Lightweight' would have done at one time, it has to be 'Ultralight' now. So is there any meaning left in it? Certainly, as long you accept that it is a relative word. It's a relative classification because it's bound to be temporary – technology moves on. At a more complex and perhaps more important level Ultralight is a kind of statement of intent, which makes the classification highly subjective and relative – relative to your objectives, to your experience, to your expectations, etc. But there are wide variations too in what people expect from their gear. For example adventure racers have a totally different take on comfort to most people and often make do with gear far too light for an ordinary backpacking trip. Same place, same temperature, but very different views of Ultralight.

His observations make excellent sense, particularly the references to experience and relativity. The other key factors in the ultralight 'revolution' are cost and durability. By and large, the lighter gear becomes, the more it costs. Being lighter doesn't necessarily mean it's more fragile (but I doubt, for instance, that current rucksacks will be in use in 50 years' time, unlike my 1961 Karrimor pack). I like his notion of a 'statement of intent': intent, that is, to move along the spectrum towards the ultralight extreme. Happily, it's up to you to decide the relative importance of all the criteria involved. Having lighter gear is no way near as important as what you use it for and what you get out of it.

Mountain marathons and adventure racing represent the pinnacle of lightweight camping demands and skills

2

ON THE MOVE

Travelling with the lightest camping gear possible offers both challenges and rewards. The key is not to compromise safety or even comfort on a longer trip. Cutting weight by leaving core kit behind and hoping for the best is not recommended. It pays to learn the basics, know your strengths and limitations and pull together a sustainable equation which includes geography, climate, weather and mode of travel. As Demetri (Coup) Coupounas, the co-founder of GoLite, says, 'Our starting point is designing and making gear and clothing that is fit for its purpose over time. We keep that at the front of our minds as we then explore ways and means of saving weight without compromising performance and to make the outdoor experience more rewarding.' Good advice to bear in mind when putting together your own kit. It's essential that whatever you decide to take on your trip does what it is designed to do and doesn't let you down. Defer the lure of shiny ultralight kit begging to be liberated from retail shelves and get some experience under your belt that can inform your choices.

Happily, the attraction of ultralight tents and sleeping bags means that there is a healthy market for pre-owned but hardly used gear. Ebay and specialist magazines are obvious sources, but don't overlook outdoor retailers' notice boards. You don't have to spend a fortune to flirt with the ultralight world. A meths stove fashioned from a beer can costs just a few pounds and weighs a handful of grams but you could buy the beer, drink it and fashion your own (not necessarily in the same evening!).

ON TWO WHEELS BY BICYCLE

Out of their saddles, into the dirt, and thereby hangs a tale

The Taming of the Shrew
William Shakespeare, 1623

Fortunately you don't need a special bike to try cycle-camping for the first time. Marketing departments will bamboozle you with the technical merits of their touring road and mountain bikes but, until you've gained some experience, just go with whatever you have to hand or can borrow. If the bug bites then you can start poring through the brochures. Set realistic goals in terms of distance and terrain but don't try to turn a holiday into an expedition. Don't train, just go.

Youngsters cycle-camping in Germany with not a parent in sight

For the first time in my life I had a 'proper' touring bicycle – light, fast, responsive – and begging for a cycle-camping trip to celebrate a significant birthday. To complement the gleaming bike the family had splashed out on front and rear panniers and a handlebar bag. All that space had to be filled, of course, so all the gear for a break tackling the Sustrans C2C (Sea to Sea) route was the work of one happy evening. Luckily I decided to go for a trial ride the next day. On the flat, the bike flew along. At the first hill, the drag of all that lightweight camping gear slowed us to a snail's pace – hopping off and pushing was the only option. It was a useful reminder to be ruthless and not to fall prey to the 'just in case' outlook on packing. The available space had been seductive, but at least the situation could be retrieved before setting off from Whitehaven and tackling the hills of the Lake District and North Pennines.

In sharp contrast, I once spent some time in the company of record-breaking cyclist Heinz Stucke (www.facebook.com/heinzstucke) whilst on his apparently never-ending world tour. His camping gear fell into the category of lightweight, but his bike and heavy-duty leather luggage, combined with his other necessities, made up a seriously heavy load. If the bike fell over, it was almost as difficult to lift as a motorbike. As he put it, 'I'm in no hurry to get anywhere, so how fast and easy is the trip is not the point.' We spent a while tracking down a workshop to weld a second set of handlebars on top of the main set. So heavy was the bike that he spent much of his time standing on the pedals or pushing up inclines. Each to their own.

Cycle-camping in Somerset my wife and I came across the more common problem of trying to find somewhere to pitch the tent each night. Intensively farmed land and few campsites could have resulted in long days and no freedom of choice. Instead, we made a point of talking to people and asking about camping opportunities with the result that useful pitches were pointed out most of the time. When it proved difficult to find one it was my wife who went to knock on doors enquiring about possibilities rather than me, a bearded sweaty monster. It worked every time.

Bike luggage

A couple of times I've packed an overnight bivvy kit in a rucksack and headed off on a mountain bike for a 'rough-stuff' trip. Knowing that I would have to carry the bike over some sections of the route, conventional panniers were pointless. But for most of us and for most of the time, carrying cycle-camping gear on our backs is not recommended – too heavy, uncomfortable and unstable.

A couple of quick-release panniers mounted on a rack over the rear wheel is the most common way of packing gear away, with the tent lashed on top of the rack; hard-sided rear-rack top bags are available. Personal items, maps, guides and snacks can be carried in a handlebar bag. Front panniers are often used for light items, but the load should not be such that it interferes with balance and steering. Tools and spares are best kept to hand in a seat-mounted 'wedge' pack.

Development of tough fabrics, welded seams and roll-top closure has made panniers effectively waterproof but it still pays to keep clothes, food and sleeping bags in additional waterproof bags. Packing away a few long zip-ties is a useful back-up if pannier attachment clips fail.

Weight distribution

If you have most of the weight on a bike loaded over the rear wheel, that wheel needs to be strong enough to cope with the strain. Bikes designed for cycle touring will be built to cope with the weight; ordinary recreational bike wheels might buckle. It's hard to spread weight around on a bike frame but a little forethought will cut back on the weight and balance it effectively.

Trailers

These have never really caught on in the UK, and those spotted on British roads are usually with Dutch or German cycle campers. Trailers are a really comfortable and stable way to haul gear and are especially useful for parents as child carriers or family-camping load haulers, leaving the youngsters load-free.

Safety on and off the road

Wearing a helmet is an obvious safety measure. Even though it may be hard to keep it on when pedalling slowly along a peaceful country road in high summer, don't lash it to the rear rack: wear it. Protective eyewear is often overlooked in the safety stakes, but even a tiny midge blown into an eye can cause a cyclist to lose control and crash.

Rarely seen but really useful in maintaining balance and control is a rear-view mirror. Mounted on the bar end, it

'I hope you're a good hand at pinning and tying strings?' Tweedledee remarked. 'Every one of these things has got to go on, somehow or other.'

Through the Looking Glass
Lewis Carroll, 1871

helps avoid the wobble in steering when looking over your shoulder before manoeuvring. Decent front and rear lights are an obvious element in safety, as well as being a legal requirement.

Legally, all new bikes have to be sold with a bell, primarily for warning pedestrians and other cyclists. A tinny tinkle will be no good for careless drivers so I have a shrill klaxon mounted on the handlebars. It's rarely used on the road and never off it. As a sensible courtesy to walkers using the bell or a cheery 'Hello!' from a distance should be the norm.

A sound bike lock is essential these days and many sites will offer secure bike storage, but it's by no means guaranteed and will have the usual disclaimers. Strangely, few campsites offer pitches with something substantial for securing bikes and locks; use your imagination and local resources.

Wet weather gear needs to be stored somewhere handy, such as on top of the rear rack.

ON TWO WHEELS BY MOTORBIKE

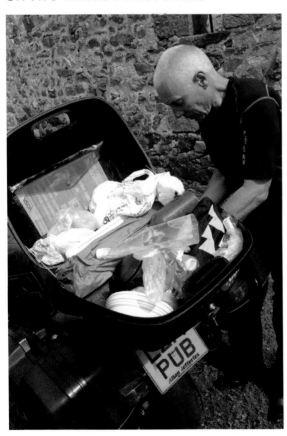

Hard to believe, but summer camping gear for two people just fitted into this rear-rack top box

Obviously, motorcyclists don't have to use their own efforts to move their machine and gear around, but that's not an open invitation to load up with masses of lightweight gear. As with cycling, there are obvious considerations of balance, control and space, as well as the need for better protection from the elements plus ease of access to and removal of bike luggage as well as its durability and security. For a long list of tongue-in-cheek tips combined with helpful hints, check out www.bmw-club.org.uk/~midland/campingtips. The difference between the two should be obvious: if not, stay at home.

At a service area off a motorway in France, I once spotted a couple of Dutch bikers sitting on folding camping chairs and enjoying a home-brewed coffee. Both were towing trailers containing camping gear and were on their way home from several weeks' touring in Spain. As one of them put it, 'Our friends think we're crazy, but we like freedom and comfort.'

In his essential guide for motorcycle touring (*Adventure Motorcycling Handbook*), Chris Scott notes, 'The Theory of Relative Space states that no matter how capacious your luggage, it will be filled to bursting point. Keep it small and you'll take little; use big containers and you'll cram them with unnecessary stuff and overload your bike.'

Whatever the size, the core choice of motorbike luggage is between soft (fabric, leather) and hard (plastic, aluminium, fibreglass, carbon fibre, steel) options. Soft luggage is usually light, cheaper, doesn't always need a rack and is not affected by vibration. On the down side, it is hard to waterproof, easier to steal from and is more susceptible to damage. Hard boxes are tough, waterproof and secure with tough racks offering quick attachment and release, though usually at a price. Against these advantages sit cost and weight. A useful theory for all lightweight campers, whatever their mode of transport.

Tank bags are useful to keep items to which you need easy access – passport, documents, wallet, camera, guides, map, snacks and glasses – and can be slung on the shoulder when off the bike. Assume it won't be waterproof.

The need for vigilance about bike security is less on a tent pitch than out and about, but there is little chance of finding a site with secure storage. Happily, modern motorbike security and a hefty lock should do the trick. If you're touring with friends lock the bikes together.

Looking at our canvas home and the bedding within, it was incredible to think that only a few minutes previously the whole lot had been contained in one small roll in a neat waterproof bag on top of our other baggage.

Two Up – by scooter to Australia
Michael Marriott, 1960

A square of alloy chequer plate is far more reliable as a side-stand base, especially on grass, than a bit of wood or the odd flat stone. Round off the corners to avoid snagging gear and clothing.

Buying cheese from the farm in the Auvergne

Many people follow the Tour de France as car or two-wheel campers. Happily, there are great alternative themes for lightweight camping trips in France with loads of small campsites and the opportunity to explore aspects of the varied character of the country and its culinary traditions. For instance, the Auvergne's Cheese Route (La Route des Fromages AOC d'Auvergne; www.fromages-aoc-auvergne.com) offers insight into the production and nature of the five main cheeses of the region.

For details see:

- Le Bleu d'Auvergne
  www.bleudauvergne.com
- Le Salers www.aoc-salers.com
- La Fourme d'Ambert www.fourme-ambert.com
- Le Cantal www.aoc-cantal.com
- Le Saint-Nectaire www.fromage-aoc-st-nectaire.com

The Maison du Saint-Nectaire – tel: 04.73.88.57.96 – is a museum-cum-cheese centre that tells the story of the history and production in a 30-minute guided tour.

Michele Velthuizen-de Vries wrote a riveting account of the experiences of touring over 16,000 miles through the USA with her husband by recumbent bike, living in a homemade tent and camping where possible.

...we finally found a dirt road off Highway 183 which led to a small white house perched on a hill. It had some land around it which looked ideal for a tent, so I went up to the house and knocked. An elderly lady came to the door and looked suspiciously at me:

'Yes?' she asked behind the screened door.

I explained in the most friendly way I could think of that we were two cyclists looking for a place to camp, ridiculous as it sounded.

'Well, I dunno...' She said reluctantly, 'I'd have to ask ma husband when he gets back...'

It was already getting dark, and who knows when this husband of hers was to return? I suggested we pitch our tent and talk to her husband after he got back. She hesitated but finally agreed.

We pitched our tent under a few trees and as soon as I saw The Huzband, I walked up to him and explained our plight. It turned out he wasn't in the least concerned about us camping on his land; he was concerned about the fact that we were camping.

'You wanna camp out here?' he said incredulously.

'Well, yes, if you don't mind that is.'

'Ah don't mind, but did you know the're rattlesnakes out there?'

Gulp.

Pedalling Unknown Paths Michelle Velthuizen-de Vries, 1985

PADDLING

In conversation, Gary and Joanie McGuffin (www.garyand joaniemcguffin.com) don't come across as one of the world's most adventurous couples, but their book *Canoeing Across Canada* details their 6000-mile journey from coast to coast. Not surprisingly, they are pretty expert in planning and sorting gear: 'Equipment had to be waterproofed yet accessible, specialized yet multipurpose and lightweight but durable. Meeting these requirements was a challenge that taxed our ingenuity to its limits... and then some.'

Although most of us will never embark on such big adventures, these words can be applied to all aspects of lightweight camping trips. My earliest canoe-camping trips were undertaken in a huge wood-and-canvas double kayak launched in the canal basin at Pontypool and paddled off in search of the headwaters of the Amazon. Waterproofed with gloss paint, it sank later in the summer and, though retrieved, was never used again. Later trips on the Severn and Ure were in an ordinary kayak with gear jammed in the

Stopping for the night on the Lot in southwest France

bow and stern. Despite the liberal use of plastic bags, everything was permanently damp. Pitches had been recce'd and arranged in advance so at least there were no irate landowners shooing us off the riverbanks.

My experience of paddling rivers for touring and camping was frustrating due to access problems, and the experience of paddling in Sweden (see below) led me off in a different direction. Curiously, the freedom enjoyed on Swedish lakes was best reflected in the freedom offered by sea kayaking at home: a few trips off the coasts of Scotland, Pembrokeshire and Northumberland were exciting and rewarding. Unfortunately, they were also demanding in terms of skills and risks, and early initiatives withered through the lack of companions, gear and knowledge. Paddling on the sea is worlds apart from sliding into a canoe on, say, the River Lot in France in bright sunshine and paddling off downstream on a three-day camping trip with no previous experience and all gear supplied. If paddling appeals and you are a novice, a trip on the Spey or Wye with everything laid on is a safe and fun way to start building a bank of knowledge.

> The wind was very strong indeed, and it was a difficult matter to get the tent up on the sand with only a few lumps of granite to fix the ropes to.
>
> *Canoeing and Camping Adventures*
> RC Anderson, 1910

THROUGH SWEDISH EYES

Paddling through inland waters in southern Sweden, the contrast between the two canoes was not immediately apparent. In portages and in camp, however, the differences were obvious. Ours was a rather heavy modern design (it felt heavy when we had to carry it), our guide Preben's was a light birch bark model made with his own hands. Even allowing for the gulf in abilities and experience, his economical paddle strokes sent him skimming over the water whilst we wallowed behind.

In camp the contrast was, if anything, even greater. It took only a few minutes for us to pitch our light two-person tent. In that time, Preben had set up a tarp, lit a small wood fire and had a brew on the go. With plenty of space in our canoe, we had packed quickly and badly; had we capsized, much of it would have been lost. We struggled at portages, and ferrying it all to the pitch above the river after tying up turned into a farce. Preben slung a modest-sized rucksack on his back, hoisted his canoe onto his shoulders and moved effortlessly from the water's edge. That day and the evening that followed was a masterclass in how to enjoy canoe camping.

As we got our petrol stove started and pulled together a two-course freeze-dried meal, we envied the mug of tea our friend was enjoying. With a real fire, he had water boiling and a frypan handy; we could heat only one pot at a time. Soon that frypan held sizzling reindeer steaks with a few parboiled potato slices lining the edges and frying slowly. With his canoe lying on its side and the tarp running over it to form a decent canopy, he would be snug, dry and comfortable whatever happened with the weather. Happily, he used a modern sleep mat and sleeping bag (if he had whittled them from a fallen branch we would have been crushed).

With the light fading, we all moved along the high riverbank to watch a beaver for a while. On top of the elk and calf seen earlier, it rounded off a superb day. Biting mozzies drove us back to the pitch where our contrasting styles became even more obvious. Without Preben, we would have been zipped up in our tent, but he stirred life into the embers of the fire, adding fallen leaves and green twigs to produce a 'smudge' fire. With the smoke drifting around us, the insect attack eased and we talked on into the night, pausing to sup tea and munch fresh pancakes. Later, as we settled down in our sleeping bags, my friend noted, 'Well, that's the way to do it then.'

So it was for him in Scandinavia, and probably North America too. Not quite so easy in the UK, maybe, but the experience taught us some useful lessons. The key was packing properly, and not thinking that we could load up the canoe without penalty. Rucksacks and sea kayaks have obvious capacity limitations, but an open Canadian canoe can swallow tons of kit.

Waterproofing

Dry bags with tightly sealed roll-top closure have revolutionised carrying camping gear, clothing and food, making packing much more flexible. Assorted colours help in keeping track of what you've packed but, if you can't rely on your memory, whip out the trusty indelible ink marker and identify them clearly.

Safety

A core item – whatever style of paddling – is a buoyancy aid or life jacket: there is no excuse for not having one. Wear it rather than slinging it on top of gear 'just in case'. Pause to reflect when that might be and how likely would be the opportunity to slip it on and fasten it up.

LIARD FIREBOX

Swiss-engineered, the Liard is a warp- and rust-free stainless steel collapsible firebox which is great for use on bank or beach when canoe or kayak camping. The idea of the firebox is well-proven and, as the name implies (the Liard river flows through Canada's Northwest Territories), the technique was popular in the tough outdoor conditions of Alaska. Using small pieces of wood in a confined space, it limits environmental damage and eliminates scarring of the ground. Easy to assemble, it takes up little space and the weight is negligible compared to the benefits (especially since a stove can be left behind). The website has an excellent series of images demonstrating function and use (see Appendix A).

Balance and access

However you're paddling, some items will be needed regularly or occasionally through the day, and others only when

A classic touring kayak design from Old Town; note the carrying toggles and deck lines for securing items such as maps

you set up camp. That sets the agenda for packing, and you'll soon learn to plan practically to avoid the frustration of a needed item being packed away in one of a number of anonymous dry bags (it'll be the least accessible, of course). If you experiment with where the weight is distributed in your canoe or kayak, you'll soon learn how it affects balance, handling and the effort needed in paddling.

A key consideration in open canoes is ensuring that nothing is lost in the event of capsizing. Kayaks with hatches make securing and keeping gear dry much easier, but needs a little forethought. Here's a rough idea for starters.

- **Front hatch** Good for food; store heavier items low down in the hull (where it's cooler), with crushable lighter items on top. It's a good place for storing cheese, vegetables and other perishables. Light, easily stuffed items such as tarp, rain gear and clothing can be stowed in the bow.
- **Cockpit** Good for items that need easy quick access on the water such as hand pump, towline, drinks, snacks, extra clothing, camera and, on the sea, flares. Make sure they are secure. Behind your seat is a good place for heavy items such as drinking water, stove, fuel and cooking pots.
- **Rear hatch** Long narrow items such as tent poles will slide into the stern along with tent, sleeping bag and sleep mat. An easily removed dry bag with clothes stowed under the hatch allows easy access to either side of the rear compartment whilst helping to stop the load shifting.

OUTDOOR CLASSIC

In the 1930s Dana Lamb and his wife June set off from San Diego, in a canoe they made themselves, on a journey that took them eventually to Central America. Their adventures have a contemporary flavour.

Into her construction we had put everything we knew, or could find out, about a sailboat, a surfboat, a canoe, and a kayak. She was a sweet little ship, and with dreams of the open sea and adventure, we christened her the Vagabunda. We could have picked no better name, for a 'vagabond' she surely was to the end of her life.

We started on our equipment as soon as she was finished. Since none of the outfitting companies could supply us with the type of equipment we thought necessary, we made our own. The equipment offered for sale was entirely too cumbersome. The lightest tent with a canvas floor that we could buy weighed eight pounds. Our homemade, insect-proof tent weighed four. Four pounds less *tent to carry enabled us to carry four pounds of something else, equally essential. The tent, sleeping bag, compact mess kit, and other gear were of our own manufacture. Into two strong, light, waterproof boxes, we stowed our food, guns, camera, films, first-aid kit, diaries, fishing gear, and repair outfit, together with the tent, sleeping bag and mess kit. Oh yes, and our cash resources as well: $4.20 carefully wrapped in a bit of oilskin.*

Enchanted Vagabonds Dana Lamb, 1938

FURTHER AFIELD

There are over 25,000 campsites in Europe, ranging from full-facility holiday parks to simple farm sites. Dramatic scenery from the fjords of Norway to Portugal's Atlantic rollers – new customs, lifestyles, history, wildlife and outdoor pursuits to explore; new food and drink to savour – all add up to a transition from 'Why go?' to 'When?' You'll need to spend more time planning a European camping holiday than you would one in the UK, but the rewards are many and varied.

There's a dramatic backdrop to the mountain holiday park of Camping Jungfrau in Switzerland's Bernese Oberland

You could take off by car with no sites booked but, at peak times (check school holiday times times with Tourist Boards and pay attention to sites' own peak period parameters) finding a site with vacancies may well be something of a lottery. Or maybe hop on a coach or take a train and then walk or pedal your way to a freewheeling camping trip. Train trips with a bike have a reputation for aggravation but I've found a little research and double-checking works wonders and train staff, mostly, happy to help. Flexibility in time of travel helps (www.nationalrail.co.uk/passenger_services/cyclists). Continental cycle travel is made much easier with the European Bike Express (www.bike-express.co.uk) that offers a flexible coach service for bikes, trikes, tandems, recumbents and their riders to France and Spain.

On the other hand, booking in to site for a few days allows for a thorough exploration of the surrounding area.

For years, relying on tourist boards and guidebooks – or word of mouth – was just about the only way to pick a site. Happily it is now easy to research location and facilities just about anywhere via the Internet. It is worth looking at the site map if pitching close to others is not your cup of tea; try to specify a pitch that suits as a condition of booking. As ever, personal recommendation heads off disappointment.

Bear in mind that just because a website has an English language version it doesn't follow that site staff will speak English, so keep a phrase book handy. Likewise, when booking, it pays to use a free translation website to send emails and interpret the replies to avoid misunderstandings.

Many sites do not take credit card payments but will expect a substantial deposit paid by electronic transfer so have a word with your bank about fees; currently, direct cross-border Internet banking transfer of personal funds is not allowed. If you're planning on touring around with sites pre-booked rather than booking a week or two at one site, the fees can mount up. Euros can be sent as cash payment, using the International Signed For service (available at post offices) to avoid bank fees, but it's hardly ideal. At peak times, sites in popular areas may well have a minimum stay requirement, often at least a week. The Camping and Caravanning Club's 'Freedom Camping' service is a flexible, low-season pay-as-you-go touring camping discount voucher scheme which takes care of booking and paying headaches.

On the road

I've used both the Automobile Association (AA) and Royal Automobile Club (RAC) for European Breakdown Cover.

For many people France is the obvious starting point for a camping holiday abroad. With over 12,000 sites on offer, there are plenty to suit all tastes and budget. It would take a lifetime of trips to explore fully the range and depth of history, culture and the regional food and wine, let alone the superb scenery and French way of life. Regional identities are strong and can form the form the basis of countless rewarding holidays. Why not explore the volcanic landscape of the Auvergne, extending from the oak trees of the Forest of Troncais to the rolling plateaux of the Cantal department? Explore the hidden byways of the Pyrenees, the Cevennes and the Jura, or enjoy the dizzy heights of the Route des Alpes by road on its way from the shores of the Mediterranean to the lofty Alpine peaks.

The official French Government Tourist Board website – www.franceguide.com – is a good starting point and offers loads of inspiration.

2

ON THE MOVE

Exploring the Lot in southwest France

Bad luck during a couple of summer breaks meant that this cover was invaluable. A guaranteed hire car meant the holiday carried on, and having the car fixed saved a lot of aggravation, particularly on the logistics and language fronts.

One August, it took the RAC three days to find a garage willing and able to carry out the gearbox repairs – peak national holiday time is no respecter of potential business, and it would have been next to impossible to sort privately. The garage was over 100 kilometres from where we were stranded (fortunately, it was where we were heading) but a low loader was arranged for our car, a taxi for the trip to pick up the hire car, and we were kept informed as to progress. Without that breakdown cover the holiday would

Carrying safety items and spares
is the law in many European
countries

have been an expensive nightmare; as it was, we were on
our way the same day.

Before starting your journey be sure to pack a first aid kit,
fire extinguisher, warning triangle, headlamp beam reflectors
and spare lamp bulbs: required by law in many countries,
it makes sense to carry them anyway. Don't forget your GB
sticker if you don't have an EU-badged number plate.

Motoring organisations recommend that you carry an
International Motor Insurance Certificate ('green card') from
your insurer. It's also useful to let them know where you
will be going, for how long, and to brush up on what to do
in the event of an accident abroad. An International Driving
Permit is not needed for Europe.

Health insurance

A European Health Insurance Card (EHIC) entitles you to
reduced cost – sometimes free – medical treatment while
you're in a European Economic Area (EEA) country and
Switzerland. The EHIC replaced the old E111 form that
you could pick up from a post office, and the easiest way
to get an EHIC is to apply online; the service is usually fast
and efficient.

The EHIC is valid for up to five years and covers state-provided medical treatment (accident or illness) you might need in the course of your holiday. The rules and regulations can be difficult to work out so it makes sense to take out travel insurance; annual multi-trip policies are usually much better value than single-trip options, and as with all insurance policies it pays to shop around.

Camping Card International

The Camping Card International (CCI) is an identity card for campers that can be used throughout Europe; note that sites in Denmark insist on a CCI. It costs a few pounds and can be bought through motoring organisations and camping clubs. Apart from some third party cover (which should be included in your travel insurance) and small discounts, the only potential advantage is in leaving it as identification at site reception instead of your passport. I've never been asked to leave my passport at any site reception, and prefer to hold on to my passport - actually, I insist. Take a couple of photocopies of your passport with you, as well as copies of other travel and insurance documents.

USEFUL WEBSITES

- **Imports and duty-free goods** www.hmce.gov.uk
- **Driving** Legal requirements, advice, breakdown cover and route planning www.theaa.com; www.rac.co.uk
- **Passports** www.ips.gov.uk
- **Travel advice** www.fco.gov.uk
- **EHIC** www.dh.gov.uk

A wonderful breakfast view looking across to Machapuchare, Nepal

3 OUT IN THE OPEN

Gissing's is a great sentiment, but one that's not always possible to endorse. One thing is for sure: whatever form 'bad weather' takes, you'll encounter it when camping (possibly in many ways over just 24 hours). The trick in being comfortable is to expect change, anticipate it and be prepared. Wherever you camp – outside of a commercial site with allocated pitches – you'll need to weigh up potential pitches. Good sites are not made, but discovered; shifting stones, stamping down vegetation and snapping tree branches is plain vandalism. It can never be condoned no matter how tired you are.

For the man sound in body and serene of mind there is no such thing as bad weather.

The Private Papers of Harry Ryecroft
George Gissing, 1903

Before setting out, make sure to check the following:
- If you have a new tent read the instructions and check you have all the bits and pieces: pitch it at home to become familiar with its idiosyncrasies.
- If using an old tent check that it is in good condition and that everything you need is in the tent bag.
- Pack a mix of pegs to cope with different ground.

Once out in the open (and before unrolling your tent), take a few minutes to consider your pitch. Everybody has their own idea of what constitutes the 'perfect pitch', but following these simple pointers will help to make the night more comfortable, wherever you are and whatever the weather:

- Pitching your tent next to running water may seem a good idea in the early evening but the sound can become irritating as the night wears on and, if the water level rises, you might get wet.
- If you have to pitch on a slope, always sleep with your head at the highest end.
- Pitch your tent so that the entrance faces away from the wind.
- Peg your tent down roughly before making adjustments to ensure it does not blow away; fix the windward side first.
- Avoid pitching at the bottom of a slope. Water run-off and cold air flowing downhill can spoil a comfortable night; that perfect valley-bottom pitch may be colder than you anticipated in the early hours.

Standard advice is to avoid pitching under a tree. Unlikely though a lightning strike or falling branch might be, the drips from above will drive you mad long after rain has stopped. In hot weather, though, leafy shade is welcome

- Do not dig a mini-moat around your tent as it damages the soil and encourages erosion. Take a little time to pick a good level pitch.
- Pitching a tent in a strong wind can test patience and tempers. Lay out pegs and poles ready to hand and peg down at least one corner of inner sheet and flysheet to help control flapping fabric and avoid frustration or damage.
- Take advantage of natural windbreaks such as hedges or walls, but resist the temptation to 'borrow' stones from dry stone walls. Strong when intact, removing stones affects their stability.
- Advice to avoid pitching under trees usually focuses on the risks of being crushed by a rogue branch. More likely is being irritated by the drip, drip, drip of water on your flysheet long after the rain has stopped. In sunnier climes, trees offer welcome shade from the sun, but take local advice before pitching.

GIVE US THE TOOLS
Bearing in mind the range of options available in terms of where to go, when and how, one set of expectations, skills and gear can hardly be expected to cope with every eventuality. Keeping an open mind helps in adapting to new

circumstances, and sound forward planning rather than optimism goes a long way to making a trip successful and rewarding. Putting off a trip because you don't have the very best equipment is truly sad. The game is about the experience, not the toys, so beg, borrow or buy what you can afford and go where you can. I put off a long-held dream of trekking in Nepal in favour of saving more money, getting more information and acquiring the best kit. In the end I just went, had a superb few months and learned how over-prepared and over-equipped one can be.

If a trip starts going wrong despite loads of research, cheery optimism will pull you through far more reliably than bad temper and moaning. It does pay, however, not to overestimate your abilities and to always keep an eye on the weather. By its very nature, lightweight camping strips away the illusion of security that domestic comforts bring. Learning how to cope and relying on our own skills and those of others loads the dice in favour of a rewarding experience in all conditions (even if it's not fully appreciated until a while later).

CAMPING IN COLD WEATHER
Generally speaking, the usual season for comfortable camping in the UK is regarded as the fairly short period from May to September. According to Swedish tent manufacturer Hilleberg, 'Technically there is hardly a difference between camping in winter and using a tent in summer.' I'm not at all sure about that optimistic statement. When you consider universal aspects such as shelter and warmth, then the devil is definitely in the detail.

Don't let snow build up on your tent – poles may snap or buckle under the weight

Detail counts when the wind blows long and cold and you want to enjoy yourself rather than just survive. Weather, location and altitude are key factors rather than time of year; when the temperature plummets the date hardly matters. Spring and autumn, let alone winter, can offer comfort challenges unknown to those who only camp in high summer.

Core elements of camping comfort from autumn through to spring are insulation, heating, location, condensation, lighting, organisation and skills. Not military precision or survival skills but a degree of forethought, sensible packing and some extra gear. Think of ways that suit you to avoid problems caused by wind, rain, cold, frost, sleet and snow and then enjoy the experience whatever the weather throws at you.

In the face of strong winds ensuring that tent pegs and guylines are up to the task is essential; extra guys may be needed, as might beefier pegs. Windbreaks around the door help to deflect chilly breezes and make it possible to cook safely, as does finding a pitch behind a wall or hedge. Keeping an airflow through the tent might seem to defeat the aim of conserving heat, but flysheets dripping with condensation are a pain (and can be a mini nightmare when it freezes). There is no sensible way of insulating a tent other than from the ground; advice to stuff the gap between inners and fly with newspaper, for instance, is laughable. Insulate the tent's interior from ground cold with a light fleece blanket. Any frost should be knocked off the flysheet each morning.

Camping by open water does have the big plus that windy conditions blow away midges and other airborne nasties though it often feels chilly

Cold will creep up from the ground and groundsheets will draw heat from you in the early hours unless you use insulation under your sleeping bag. A sleeping bag liner will add loads of warmth to a bag, but 4am on a December night is not the time to find out your bag isn't up to the mark. If planning to camp in winter, make sure you have plenty of insulation under your sleeping bag as well as using one that will cope with the low temperatures. It's easy to go to extremes and suggest a suitable sleeping bag for UK winter camping: a bag designed for Himalayan climbing and costing several hundred pounds, for example, should cope easily, but that's not practical for most of us. The only way of finding out your own limits and comfort zone is to 'give it a go' (though the garden is far safer for early trials than the Scottish mountains).

All campers should be aware of the potential dangers of carbon monoxide poisoning and fire resulting from cooking inside a tent. Bite the bullet, wrap up warm and don't give in to the temptation to zip up the doorways, turn up the burners and disappear in a fug of steam and poison. Organisation and forward planning come into their own when cooking out of season. Quick, hot, filling grub is just the ticket. Avoid anything fancy or that may need long cooking. With hours of daylight shortening lighting becomes far more important, so it pays to invest in a reliable head torch and, maybe, a small lantern.

After a long day spent reaching and crossing the Cairngorm plateau, it was a relief to head downhill to our planned pitch for the night. Despite the energy-sapping deep snow, the day had been glorious – as had the weather. Warm, dry and comfortable in layers of high-tech clothing, we were determined to set up camp long before it got dark. As it happened, short daylight hours and slow progress meant we ran out of time, and we shuffled up and down in the gloaming making a level base for the tent in the deep snow with a snow deck for easy access. Having used ice axes to shift the top few inches of snow, we had a firm base with low walls to deflect any breeze that might develop. Ice axes and a couple of chunky snow stakes secured main guylines, flysheet valances were packed down with snow, whilst light stuff sacks were filled with more snow and buried as anchors to complete securing the guylines. Using a variety of methods reduced the potential effect of a disastrous change in the weather as we slept.

Moonrise now flooded the nearby frozen lochan and snow-clad slopes making head torches redundant. Tasks were split through long practice. One to collect water – carefully – while the other spread out a light fleece blanket to cover the whole groundsheet, opened up the full-length sleep mats, laid out and fluffed up sleeping bags and assembled the stove. It was the work of only a few minutes, soon followed by hot blackcurrant laced with a tot of brandy. A review of the day accompanied the heating of the main meal and the obligatory competition to outdo each other with snacks and starters (livening up freeze-dried meals with extras adds key dimensions to winter fare). The head chef needed a head torch to cook and serve the food but, despite the cold, we sat outside, relishing the hot taste sensations.

A wee dram and a few squares of chocolate rounded off the meal but, through long experience, we gave coffee a miss. It is no fun struggling out of sleeping bag and tent through the night to empty an aching bladder. Unfortunate pee bottle accidents had ruled that option out.

Pot and bowl cleaning was followed by heating up more water to rinse feet, wash hands and fill metal water bottles. As long as the water was not boiling, these made excellent hot water bottles thrust into the depths of the down-filled bags along with fleece jackets, trousers, gloves and socks. The clothes would be warm for the morning and the water handy for getting a brew underway before leaving our down cocoons. Base layers and hats were essential nightwear. Boots stayed by the door doubling as handy cup holders and stashes for head torches, glasses and lighter. In the morning they would be cold and stiff, but this was not the Arctic and they would have warmed up on our feet by the time we had breakfast, packed up and moved on. It was time to embrace the sleep of the bone-weary.

By way of contrast, meeting up with friends on a commercial campsite for a series of winter day walks had two key differences. Whilst the 'getting ready for bed' routine was similar, a larger tent, handy showers and toilets, and the shelter (plus facilities) of a friend's much-maligned caravan turned the experience into camping in the winter rather than true wild winter camping – still fun.

3

OUT IN THE OPEN

It doesn't have to be the depths of winter for temperatures to drop sharply overnight and for frost to form on a tent flysheet

Cold weather tips

- Always knock snow off clothing before entering the tent to help keep the interior dry, and leave footwear under the fly to avoid damaging the groundsheet.
- Wearing layers of lighter clothing instead of one chunky jacket allows you to adjust easily the amount of insulation and thus warmth. This flexibility helps in keeping dry, both from weather and sweat.
- Feather and down sleeping bags will not keep their insulation values when damp, so be disciplined about looking after natural fills. Replacing the stuff sack supplied with a waterproof dry bag will reduce the risks.
- A mummy-style bag is warmer than a rectangular as there is less space for your body to heat and it wraps snugly around your head and shoulders. Try not to sleep with your head under the covers as this increases humidity in the bag, reducing the insulation properties of the fill.
- Try to air out your sleeping bag and tent whenever you can. Perspiration and warm breath condense in the tent at night and the moisture will reduce warmth.
- Wear a beanie or woolly hat to bed in order to reduce heat loss through your head.

- Wear your base layer clothing in bed and keep the clothes you plan to wear the following day inside your bag overnight.
- A sleeping bag liner will improve the bag's warmth significantly.
- Insulate yourself from the ground as much as possible to avoid the cold drawing heat away; a good rule of thumb is two to three times the insulation below you as over you. Remember that you'll be flattening the insulation under you.
- Put a hand warmer (in a sock) or warm water bottle at the foot of your sleeping bag before getting into it.
- A little exercise before settling down for the night will raise your body heat and help to warm your bag.
- It usually takes longer to cook food in cold weather so plan accordingly.
- Torch batteries are affected by cold; you can revive a dead battery by warming it up in your hands or next to your skin – if you can stand it. Wrap batteries in a sock and place them in your bag with you overnight when temperatures drop really low.

CAMPING IN HOT WEATHER

This book is neither an expedition guide nor an encyclopae-dia of all conceivable aspects of lightweight camping gear. Hot weather might be wet (as in tropical rain forest) or it might be dry (as in what most of us hope for) but does not necessarily mean desert. So this section won't be debating the finer points of hammocks or mesh inner tents. Instead it will cover those bright sunny conditions which we might reasonably expect to encounter in and on the fringes of southern Europe and, every now and then, in the UK.

Most of us will embrace the idea of camping in balmy weather caressed by a gentle breeze. In reality, it can be easier to get comfortable in cold weather than in hot. A small single-skinned (waterproof fabric; no flysheet) tent used in Slovenia one summer turned into a mobile sauna on hot still nights, making sleeping impossible even with the doors tied open. It was the same tent we had used in Iceland and, having failed in hot, cold and wet weather, it was even-tually cut up to make stuff sacks and an early tarp tent.

On one camping trip in Turkey shade was the key factor in picking a site, whilst tales of Ottoman horned vipers had us choosing an insect mesh inner in our pyramid-style tent. It seemed unlikely that any snake would unzip the inner and join us for warmth. We do enjoy hot weather in this country and a particularly glorious summer saw us moving the tent from the lee of a hedge on a small site in Cornwall

Obviously hot and with no shade available, this pitch benefits from an early morning breeze – but it's time to pack up and move on

to an exposed pitch near the summit of a small hill with wonderful views and a welcome breeze that blew steadily through the night.

Sewn-in groundsheets and modern tent styles mean that the only ventilation option usually available is to leave the doorway open and hope that any little ventilation 'tunnels' in the flysheet will allow some airflow. Unless you're planning a long trip in a hot climate, there is no need to buy desert-ready camping gear. Plan for the usual conditions you encounter and adapt what you've got when necessary.

Hot weather tips

- Shade of any sort is useful in trying to keep the temperature down inside the tent.
- Unlike camping in other conditions a breeze can be very welcome, so pitching in an exposed position may be the answer.
- Dark colours soak up heat, so green flysheets are not the best choice.
- Insect-proof mesh screens on inner doorways allow a degree of ventilation without tent occupants being bitten to distraction.
- A full-length sleeping bag zip allows flexibility in both getting to sleep (when it can be unzipped to reduce temperature) and staying warm in the early hours of morning.
- A tarp offers welcome shade for cooking and eating even if you plan on sleeping in your tent.
- Make sure you have plenty of water and drink regularly.
- Dress to protect yourself against the sun; use sunscreen and wear a hat.

- Ultra-violet rays in bright sunshine, especially at higher altitudes, can wreak havoc on nylon flysheets causing degradation of the fabric. Most tent flysheet material will have UV inhibitors, and Nikwax produces a Tent & Gear Solarproof spray which has the benefit of blocking the effects of UV and waterproofing the fabric, claiming to double the effective life of gear (see Appendix A).

HEAT ILLNESSES

It is important to know how to deal with heat-related health problems when camping. Be aware of the following symptoms:

- **Heat cramps** Severe cramps in the legs and abdomen caused by losing too much water and salts by sweating. Drink plenty of water and/or rehydration solution and rest in shade.
- **Heat exhaustion** Excessive sweating, dilated pupils, dizziness, blurred vision, symptoms of shock such as cold, clammy skin, shallow breathing, vomiting and even unconsciousness. Rest the patient in a cool place with feet elevated and loosen clothing. Unless vomiting, give plenty of water and rehydration solution. If the patient is unconscious, place in the recovery position and seek medical help urgently.
- **Heat stroke/sunstroke** Potentially life-threatening: the body's temperature rises far above normal. Unlike heat exhaustion, the skin is extremely hot and flushed (but can also be dry or sweaty). Possible symptoms include noisy breathing, rapid and weakening pulse, restlessness, headache, fatigue, dizziness, nausea, vomiting, convulsions and unconsciousness. Summon medical help and try to cool the patient: remove outer clothing, cover with wet sheets and sponge down with cool water, especially around neck, armpits and groin.

3

OUT IN THE OPEN

A basecamp by the Indian Ocean under fierce sunshine: two tents sharing the welcome shelter offered by a garden gazebo while enjoying the cool breeze off the sea

CAMPING IN WET WEATHER

Wind and rain; they seem to go together

AND WHEN IT REALLY RAINS...

The prospect was not encouraging. We'd been dropped off in the middle of Iceland by a walking tour operator's 4WD bus and left to our own devices, so we had to walk out. No problem: that was always the plan. Fording dozens of streams had also been considered, but even at our most pessimistic we had not anticipated never-ending torrential rain: we were embarking on a crash course in coping with wet weather. Fortunately, there was no wind to speak of and it wasn't all that cold in July. The problem was the tent – too small, no storage space, leaking seams, porous groundsheet – and, being a single-skin proofed nylon model, it streamed inside with condensation. It was all we could afford and we had to live with it. At home it had seemed like a bargain and a weekend in the Cheviots to try it out the week before had shown up some limitations, but far from all. However, this was the real world. The tent was all we had and it was going to take us about six days to reach our goal of a remote youth hostel and the possibility of a ride back to Reykjavik. With no trees or hedges for shelter, we were exposed to the landscape – and the rain.

Having accepted that reality we had to make a plan, and as the miles unfolded it came together. Considering the months of scheming that had gone into the trip, it was a rueful duo that faced the dismal failure of that scheming on the ground. Happily, the views were grand and the land felt wild and remote despite the rough tracks we followed. With only the odd bird for company, we strode on and worked out how to be as comfortable as possible. (In fact we burst out laughing: it was either that or sob in frustration at the combination of fast-flowing bitterly cold streams and, in sharp contrast, warm heavy rain.)

With no tent flysheet there was nowhere to cook or park the rucksacks overnight. With feather-filled sleeping bags, we couldn't let them get too wet if we wanted to sleep comfortably. At least the virtually 24-hour light of a northern summer meant we didn't have to cope with the dark. The attraction of bothy-based walking holidays was becoming much clearer by the hour. A tentative routine emerged which became the pattern for the following days.

We walked until we were really tired (walking in the rain was far better than hanging about in it). Having picked a site, the first job was to pitch the tent. As it was fastened to the lid of my rucksack, nothing else got wet and it took no time to get it pitched. With doors at each end, we each knelt at an entrance and helped each other to lay out sleeping mats and sleeping bags on top of an all-weather blanket. That dealt, more or less, with shelter and sleeping needs.

Everything we needed for our main meal was laid out in a doorway and the kitchen was next. Wedging our rucksacks upright, we draped a survival bag over them to create a sheltered space for the stove with open access on two sides, and placed another survival bag on the ground to sit on whilst we cooked and ate in our water-proofs. There was no incentive to hang around, so once the food had been devoured it was time for bed. The budget tent had tape closure to the flimsy doors and, even without a breeze, rain drifted through them. Our answer was to strip off, thrusting boots and clothes into rucksacks and leaning them across the doorway at one end. Skin being both breathable and waterproof, we took it in turns to roughly dry off as we crawled into the tent at the other end. One of us turned back to the entrance to roughly shake the water off our waterproof jackets. Zipped up, they were pulled over the feet of the sleeping bags to deflect the worst of the rain and condensation. We settled down to sleep; despite the light, that was no problem.

In the morning the routine was reversed. As there was no let-up in the downpour, everything got damper each day and our comfort level dropped. At the same time, our learning curves steepened and a few days later we felt we knew how to cope and what to do next time. Probably the key lessons were to opt for a big tarp if we couldn't afford a reliable lightweight tent and to buy synthetic fill sleeping bags.

In North Wales later that year in we sat in a larger tent (borrowed) with a full waterproof flysheet. As darkness fell so did the rain, and it grew heavier by the hour. In the early hours we were woken by a strange sensation. It took a while to work out that it was rain run-off from the slope behind us flowing under the tent. The value of a sound groundsheet was really appreciated.

Wet weather tips

- A tent that pitches flysheet first has a couple of advantages: the inner doesn't get wet and you can get out of the rain quickly by diving under the flysheet to get sorted and cook or enjoy a lunch break.
- Sodden ground won't hold tent pegs as securely so, when tightening guylines, double-check pegs.
- Side guylines not only add stability but also help to keep condensation on the inside of the flysheet from wetting the inner.

Nylon stretches and sags when wet so be prepared to adjust guylines. Keeping flysheets taut helps to avoid wind damage and brushing against damp walls.

- Don't be tempted to cook inside the tent – it's not worth the high risk of fire and carbon monoxide poisoning.
- Keep wet gear out of the tent at all costs.
- If you think you're going to be in for really wet weather, pack a little sponge. It weighs next to nothing and will make short work of mopping up water inside the tent.
- Think ahead and try not to keep popping in and out of the tent.
- Avoid likely run-off areas from waterlogged ground higher up.

Shelter from the storm

Sometimes wet weather becomes overwhelming and you need to take a break. On a memorable cycle-camping trip in East Anglia, yet another deluge drove us to seek sanctuary in a bus shelter. The respite was more than just welcome and brief. After cooking a meal, we made ourselves comfortable, christened the shelter 'Bike Bothy' and stayed the night. Flexibility and common sense once again won out over vague notions of principle. On another trip, after several days spent paddling in the rain on the Wye, the offer of shelter under a carport of a riverside house was welcome. The freestanding dome tent meant that the concrete floor was no obstacle to pitching. By bedtime the breeze had dried the previous three days' rain from tent, sleeping bags and clothes. In Corsica, a truly foul day ended happily when we were offered the veranda of a school to sleep on out of the rain. That sympathetic teacher opened up the school early in the morning to let us shower and produced coffee and a couple of *pains au chocolat* for breakfast. Never underestimate the generosity of strangers.

CAMPING NEAR WATER

Camping in the Lake District by a small stream running into a small tarn, we joked about flooding. Several hours later we found ourselves packing up in heavy rain as the stream burst its banks and we splodged away to higher ground. It was a useful reminder that assuming that nothing is likely to go wrong usually ends in tears. Such assumptions are usually linked to the wishful thinking that accompanies tired bodies and minds.

Happily, not all camping by water has a negative association. On a clifftop on the Cleveland Way one summer our tents were, technically, by the sea, benefiting from a brisk onshore breeze and a superb sunrise the following morning. In contrast, an overnight pitch on a grassy knoll along the Northumberland coast had waves at high tide crashing onto

I found, sure enough, a perfect campsite: a small, level, grass-carpeted ledge, just far enough from the creek to avoid any danger of my polluting it but close enough for easy water supply and for music.

The Secret Worlds of Colin Fletcher Colin Fletcher, 1989

the beach just yards away. The remnants of a small beach fire, made the evening before below the high-water mark of debris, had been swept away along with sleepy cobwebs.

Think twice before camping right next to water

In considering camping by water, it pays to split the options into still water, running water and the sea. Plus, of course, the context: there's a world of difference between camping near a fast-flowing mountain stream or by a sluggish mature river or canal.

Research, as ever, pays dividends. Planning a Munro-bagging trip to Loch Mullardoch (a reservoir formed by damming a remote valley), the map showed level ground about halfway along the lochside that looked suitable for a basecamp for a few days. Fortunately, we checked with the chap who was whisking us up the loch by boat. Our proposed pitch was boggy and peat riven with deep gullies and was, apparently, a midgie nightmare. The alternative suggested, on a patch of level higher ground beyond a tarn, was firm, well drained, midge-free, offered easy access to fresh water and a safe area for sanitation needs. Result.

Without doubt the strangest camping by water enjoyed over the years happened in Sweden. The combination of building a log raft and floating down a river, camping each night over a week or so, was irresistible. Enthusiasm for the Huckleberry Finn experience was tempered by being well aware of Scandinavia's hordes of biting insects. A sailing friend offered a small anchor which, secured to a length of light rope, allowed us to moor in mid-stream, avoiding the biting legions. We plastered dried riverbed mud over the logs as a base for cooking over a real fire and as a floor for sleeping on board, with no shortage of water for endless brews.

Restrictions on river and bankside access in the UK prompted a sustained interest in sea kayaking with the opportunities to explore more remote – or at least not well frequented – areas of coast and find some solitude. The robust appearance of so much of our coastline belies its fragility, and the need to be aware of the impact of camping, particularly in beachside dunes.

Near water tips
- Safely disposing of human waste at a distance from the lake or river (30–50m) is the priority.
- On the coast, bury waste above the high-water mark.
- Avoid camping in sand dunes and never damage beachside vegetation – it may look tough but is far from resilient when walked over.
- As rivers rise, so does the water table and the likelihood of damp seeping through a worn groundsheet.
- Be aware of wildlife and enjoy viewing it without any disturbance.
- Bear in mind that waterside pitches may be cold and poorly drained, as well as full of insect life.
- As well as rising steadily as rain falls, mountain streams can burst their banks without warning in a flash flood.

CAMPING IN THE MOUNTAINS

I have always been drawn to mountains and have a fairly flexible view as to what can be called one. It's easy to spot the Himalaya, Alps and Cairngorms as mountains, less easy to include the Cheviots, for instance, but for the purposes of this book hill ranges count as mountain country. Camping in the Alwinton valley on the fringes of those Border hills, a pitch had been chosen carefully to avoid the potential hazards of flood and environmental damage. What had been seriously overlooked was the funnel effect of the steep valley sides on the wind. In the middle of the night it felt like we were in a wind tunnel, and we spent around three hours holding onto the poles at each end of the tent. By morning, shelter from wind had shot up the list of considerations for a good pitch.

Sometimes you weigh up all the factors involved in a sound pitch and then ignore them (not lightly, of course, but for good reason). Having carried a tent for many days in Nepal there was no way I wasn't going to spend some time camping, despite the charms of trekkers' lodges. Exposed to the afternoon wind that howled down the Kali Gandaki gorge from Mustang and suffering from relentless sunshine, there was no water to be found in the bare landscape and the pegs scarcely penetrated the hard-baked ground as I set up camp below Muktinath. Despite all the alleged negatives, it still counts as one of the best campsites ever with spectacular sunsets and the Dhauligiri massif for company across the valley.

Far less dramatic were the nights enjoyed crossing North Wales and the Scottish Highlands, alternating tent and bivvy bag depending on the weather and location. With camping as an integral part of both trips rather than just a means

Mist, wind and rain should always be expected in mountainous country

to an end, it was easy to stop when a good spot became apparent, even if the earlier plan had been to walk on further. Watching the way light – sun and moon – changes the perception of the mountains is an essential element in being there, and even wet days can be rewarding.

With no accumulation of experience, embarking on a winter backpack across the Cairngorm mountains is not recommended. At times, the plateau offers arctic conditions which make mincemeat of inexperienced walkers and campers. Better by far to start off by camping in the valleys from spring to autumn, building confidence and ability before heading off into the hills. Backpacking guidebooks are a good starting point for route-planning options, as are National Park rangers.

Mountain camping tips
- Camping under cliffs or at the base of scree brings with it the risk of bouncing rocks hitting the tent.
- Level sites might be more difficult to find, so be prepared to adapt your notions of the ideal site.
- Protection from the wind is a higher priority than a lovely view; make sure your tent is pitched as securely as possible.
- Weather changes quickly in mountain country, so always keep an eye on what's happening.
- Potential pitches may be thin on the ground so look ahead, read your map and the country closely, and don't leave stopping too late.
- It might be difficult to peg out your tent securely, so carry a few metres of light cord to help in making use of rocks and boulders.
- Lightning is more of a potential hazard in mountain country.
- Sunshine can do more than leave mountain travellers suffering from sunburn, as ultraviolet rays can cause damage to tent fabric: see 'Camping in hot weather'.
- If you have no experience of camping in snow then finding out about it in mountains is not recommended; develop your skills in the valley first.
- In high altitudes the boiling point of water is lowered and thus the speed of cooking reduced, increasing fuel consumption. At sea level, the boiling point of water is 212°F (100°C). As a guide, the temperature decreases by 1°F for every 540 feet of altitude gained (roughly 1°C for every 300 metres). It's all about atmospheric pressure. Think about how a pressure cooker speeds up cooking times; altitude in the open air has the reverse effect.

- Temperature decreases with altitude: higher ground can be subject to vicious winds.
- Collecting water from a spring bubbling up to the surface high in the mountains is an idyllic way to meet drinking and cooking needs. Sadly, drinking from an apparently clean rushing mountain stream is no guarantee that the water is potable; there really could be a dead sheep in the water upstream and out of sight. All good outdoor shops carry a range of effective water treatment solutions. Combining your choice with common sense, observation and carrying enough to tide you over should solve all problems.

Extreme camping: no water; no shade; strong winds; rocky ground; no comfort – but great view overlooking the Kali Gandaki Gorge on the Annapurna trail, Nepal

4 SHELTER

> The main thing in hike-camping is to select equipment of the lightest weight. At one time such an outfit would have weighed not less than 24lb; but nowadays, since manufacturers of camping equipment have specialised in producing lightweight outfits suitable for carrying on the back, the full weight of the kit need not exceed 14lb or so.
>
> *The Rucksack Way* Arthur Sharp, 1934

Many people think that the concept of lightweight camping is a modern trend that takes advantage of advances in material technology and computer-aided design, but in reality trimming the weight of camping gear has been on the agenda for years. TH Holding, one of the pioneers of recreational camping in the 1900s, developed a tent made of silk that weighed just 11oz, excluding pegs and pole/s.

As the weight-saving obsession gathered pace a few years ago, more and more cautionary tales came my way. Almost all were connected with the weather. Carrying no spare clothing, using a light down-filled sleeping bag and sleeping under a flimsy tarp can be a joy in settled dry weather. When those conditions turn more hectic, the weaknesses inherent in ultralight kit become apparent. As is so often the case in outdoor pursuits, we have to hope for the best and prepare for the worst. Wishful thinking by a couple of guys I met on the Pennine Way resulted in them being cold, wet and miserable – in August. As one of them wryly put as we ran them to a railway station, 'This is not California and it's been tough; we don't really know what we're doing.' It was their first long-distance trip, and their experience underlines the need to balance the equation of seasons, weather, terrain, gear, skills and experience.

Learning the hard way seems to be axiomatic in this area and many people have found their single-skin lightweight tent impossible to live in after several days' heavy rain, some even confessing to seeking out campsites and cooking in the wash block. My early trips were often nearly ruined by carrying too much gear – 'just in case'. Excess clothes were posted home when tackling Wainwright's Coast to Coast walk; cutting out mozzie nets to shave weight

Holding's 'Gypsy' design resembles a modern toilet tent, so he was either very short or slept upright! Perhaps not, but this highlights a key aspect of lightweight gear: 'Any fool can be uncomfortable.' Trim, trim, trim… and eventually comfort and safety are sacrificed.

Low weight and packed size of gear frees up space in your rucksack for food – or just to make each day's travel easier

Sometimes the cheapest and healthiest way to cut down on weight is to go on a diet rather than spend money on a lighter piece of kit.

...if you enter the wilderness unprepared, without adequate food or equipment, you'll probably fail to appreciate it.

Vagabonding in the USA
Ed Buryn, 1980

bitterly regretted when cycle camping in a midge-infested Scottish summer. Happily I've rarely made the same mistake twice, and usually follow local advice. Turning up in Turkey to wander along the Lycian Way one September, my tent and fleece jacket were left behind and extra water carried instead after a new friend had rummaged through my pack and discarded unnecessary items.

Gear manufacturers keep designing better and better 'mousetraps', but try not to burden yourself with loads of lightweight stuff. I once met a backpacker in Scotland who was carrying two stoves (in case one broke) but who had bought sandwiches for his first night's meal – madness. The less your basic gear weighs, the more food you can carry, which can extend the length of time you spend outdoors and the distance you cover (or simply allow you to enjoy bigger meals).

The main factor affecting the amount and type of gear you need is likely to be the weather, both in terms of season and the vicarious patterns found in mountain regions. Add in budget, your own ideas on comfort and durability, plus the length of time that you plan to be away and you end up with a complex broth. It is fun, though, to scheme. Making up detailed lists for future trips, realistic or fantasy, with actual budgets or no consideration of cost can help focus thoughts and plans. And it is not only attitude, experience and materials that have influenced gear trends – a mobile phone and reading glasses now feature in my checklists.

If you are new to the game, spend slowly and carefully as your experience increases. Rushing out to buy the latest, lightest gear does not guarantee a comfortable trip, even if the photos look cool.

Think about:
- Buying well-made durable gear that will give good service
- Not buying more than you really need
- Taking care of your gear
- When you have finished with it, passing it on or recycling rather than binning it.

TENTS

A tent appears to be a simple piece of kit offering protection from rain, sun, insects and wind. If only it was that simple! A common question heard in outdoor shops is, 'What's the best tent on the market?' So many factors come into play for each individual purchase that it is impossible to recommend one tent for all purposes and people. Inevitably, any purchase will be a compromise involving price, purpose, personal preference, durability, weight and availability. Have a think about what you want beforehand.

It is really easy to baffle yourself with brochure jargon and to become obsessed with shaving grams off the weight of your tent. Enjoy the agonising and weighing up of options; it costs nothing and you'll learn a lot. When it comes to parting with hard cash, however, take a step back. Be honest about what you are likely to do with your new tent before committing to an expensive purchase. You might want to think twice about spending hundreds of pounds on an ultra-lightweight model if you will only use it for a few nights each summer after a short walk to your pitch. On the other hand, if you are planning a demanding winter backpacking traverse of Scotland, make sure the tent you choose is up to the task and as light as you can afford.

As a reliable way of defining what a tent can cope with from the elements, a rating by season is a rough guide only. It becomes almost irrelevant when you consider the context, weather and altitude you're likely to encounter. Camping in Iceland at sea level in spring is considerably more demanding than sea level in Turkey in the autumn.

Before buying a two-person tent for a two-week trek with your partner or best friend, get into the tent together. Imagine what it will like at dusk on a wet windy evening with supper yet to be prepared, wet clothes, full rucksacks and no sign of the rain stopping. Most manufacturers are rather optimistic in their assessment of the space needed for two or three people to live in a tent comfortably and not fall out with each other so take time to check it out. Of course, more room usually means greater weight, but splitting the load eases the pain.

No one tent is ever ideal. How can it be?

Backpacking in Britain
Robin Adshead, 1974

4

SHELTER

81

A lateral double sloping design which aims to maximise useful internal space

Tent designs

Tent designs have become ever more complex, incorporating aspects of different basic styles into hybrids that weave advantages together. Happily, they are all easy to pitch and stem from four key options. Almost all will have a waterproof outer or flysheet and an inner tent with sewn-in groundsheet, though single-skin tents made with breathable fabrics are available.

- **Dome** Simple, popular, aerodynamic and stable, they are designed to shed wind, rain and snow.
- **Geodesic** Offers excellent structural strength through the use of intersecting poles to form a self-supporting structure with loads of internal space. On an Ullswater paddling trip a borrowed mountain expedition tent reinforced the benefits of a geodesic design. A howling gale had little effect on the tent whilst others were bent out of shape and suffered snapped poles. The penalties were weight and bulk, but fortunately we were car-based on that occasion.
- **Hoop or Tunnel** Usually available in two- and three-hoop styles these are quick to pitch and offer plenty of space inside; having a large porch they are popular with cyclists.

A dome design is quick to pitch and offers plenty of internal space

This geodesic inner tent with extra crossed poles ensures stability in awful weather and plenty of internal space

- **Ridge** The classic tent as drawn by most children, including any tent with fore and aft upright or sloping poles – also known as an 'A' frame – possibly with a horizontal pole running between them. In backpacking tents the back upright is usually lower than the one at the entrance, reducing the overall weight.

Most lightweight tents have one entrance, with the flysheet forming a porch useful for cooking and gear storage. The insect mesh screen on the inner door helps with ventilation and enables you to watch the world outside without being eaten alive. Extended porches on many designs make for more comfortable tent living, especially in bad weather, with more flexible storage, drying and cooking options. Pockets on the inner tent and a clip-on hanging gear hammock in the inner tent ensures that small items such as a torch, glasses, radio or earplugs are not mislaid. Flysheet-first pitching enables campers to erect quick shelter before fitting the inner, or to use the flysheet alone.

Hoop designs with an entrance porch are popular in tents used for lightweight car camping

A mini-hoop design with plenty of access

A large extended porch offers loads of storage and cooking space for two people

Key elements
Key design elements to look out for include ventilation, stability, usable space and weight, plus cooking and storage options. Condensation is a potential problem in all designs

Really easy to pitch, hoop or tunnel designs usually need more side guylines for stability in crosswinds

A modern interpretation of the classic sloping ridge design

83

This truly lightweight design combines a hoop with a sloping ridge to give stability, storage room and shelter for cooking

with a waterproof non-breathable flysheet. In bad weather, with all zips closed, there is little chance of beating it. In more settled weather a degree of ventilation is possible by using the two-way zips. However, compared to being outside in the rain, condensation is a minor inconvenience and a fact of camping life. Far more important is stability, particularly in high winds. Fabric, cut, poles and guylines all contribute to maintaining the integrity of design and comfort.

All designs represent a balance between certain elements: weight versus space and cost versus quality, for instance. Floor plans do not give the full picture of usable space, nor what the tent feels like when inside; headroom is key. I've given up on tents that had a large floor area but that, through a combination of fabric and cut, had the inner tent sagging onto face and feet through the night. It felt like being in a quilt cover rather than a tent, and reinforced the need to see a tent pitched before buying.

A mesh inner door allows ventilation and views without hordes of biting midges running riot

It is difficult to work out cost/benefit advantages from brochures and technical jargon alone. Apparent anomalies in weight and price might be explained by the quality of fabrics and components, which is when looking over a tent that has been pitched in the rain for a couple of days can be illuminating. Chatting with other campers will give more rounded views on manufacturers and designs than those gained at exhibitions.

It is hard now to find groundsheets that are not sewn-in to the inner tent. Obvious pluses are cutting out draughts and stopping creepy crawlies from invading your space; the downside is that when they start leaking they cannot really be satisfactorily re-proofed.

Single-skin tents can offer significant weight savings, but I have not yet found one that suits. Whether made from waterproof breathable materials, such as Gore-Tex, or non-breathable proofed nylon or polyester, condensation has always been a pain, as have windy nights spent wondering how long the tent would survive.

Extra clip-on storage space not only keeps items such as hats, gloves and socks handy but also gives them a chance to dry

Materials

Most campers would prefer to blend into the landscape rather than stick out as an orange blot; green and blue fly-sheets offer a soft light inside. Most lightweight flysheets and inners are made of nylon fabric or harder wearing polyester; for groundsheets, a slightly heavier fabric is often used for better abrasion resistance. The susceptibility of groundsheets

Muted colours aren't about camouflage but about not sticking out

Sealing tent seams is an easy maintenance task with the right material

to damp soaking through from damage or wear by abrasion has resulted in the popularity of 'footprints' – tougher material laid on the ground under the inner tent. This adds weight as well as extending durability, so neatly falls into the pattern of every benefit having an associated cost.

Flysheets and groundsheets are coated to make them completely waterproof, while inner tents use a more open-weave uncoated fabric for breathability. Polyurethane (PU) is the most common coating used, though is more expensive, and highly slippery silicone elastomer does allow even lighter fabrics to be proofed without sacrificing strength. As these coatings are non-breathable, condensation of the body moisture vapour that forms needs to be tackled by adequate ventilation.

Pegs, poles and guylines

As a general rule, the more your tent costs the lighter and stronger the poles are likely to be. Most poles are now linked via elastic shockcord making pitching much quicker; flexible aluminium poles are lighter and harder wearing than fibre-glass, and those made from carbon fibre lighter and stronger still – at a price. Whatever your poles and however they are attached to the tent (sleeves or clips), the key to hassle-free pitching is to know where they go. Sounds easy – and in one-person designs it usually is. Geodesic and hoop tents benefit from colour-coding poles and locations. If not done by the manufacturer, then adding your own is useful – insulating tape does the job. Remember that once in tension, poles seem really strong. Lying on the ground, however, they can be damaged or even snapped, so take care when pitching. Similarly, try to avoid holding on to them for balance.

You will get enough simple pegs with your purchase to pitch the tent in firm ground with no breeze. Buy some extras: Y-shaped toughened aluminium pegs are probably the most versatile, but there is no shortage of options on the market. Pegs are made from all sorts of materials (steel, wood, aluminium, alloy, carbon fibre, titanium and plastic) in an ingenious variety of designs, some even with luminous ends. As these humble items are the tent anchors, they should be looked after – make the effort occasionally. Learn from experience what suits you, your tent and different terrain before lashing out on dozens of pegs for all eventualities. One of my best buys (in a sale) was four alloy snow stakes. Hardly ever used in snow, they are superb in sand.

Although plastic pegs are cheap and tempting, they are easily damaged in hard ground and should be avoided.

Although tents come with their own guylines, I like to pitch a tent at home and juggle them before using it on a trip. Key guylines are double-checked; optional ones are added in advance on the basis that, when needed, there will no time to find and add them. Different colours help in identifying key guylines and luminous cord helps to spot them at night – not so much for adjusting them as not tripping over them. Metal or plastic, easy-to-use guyline adjusters rely on friction to loosen or tighten the cords as required. Remember that nylon guylines will stretch when wet so will need adjustment in rain and damp conditions.

Awnings and windbreaks

Once the preserve of caravanners, awnings for tents suitable for car-based touring and longer-term basecamps have become popular in recent years. They add extra shelter from rain and sun, avoiding the need to stay in the tent. Being self-contained, they are flexible and, used in conjunction with a windbreak, give a lot more usable outdoor living space.

Long tall windbreaks made from nylon with fibreglass poles can transform cooking and eating outdoors for car campers. Apart from the protection from the wind, they also ensure a degree of privacy. At present, no manufacturers offer a really lightweight windbreak, but a small simple one can be fashioned from ripstop nylon and cycle spokes that, when set around a light tent or bivvy bag, really does stop the wind causing cooking problems. Happily, it's usually possible to find some form of natural windbreak and pitch in the lee of it.

Add or change guylines to suit your personal preference and where and when you plan to be camping

A windbreak offers privacy as well as shelter

Bivvy bags

Known variously as a 'bivvy' or 'bivi', bivouac bags offer very lightweight reliable protection, usually for one person, as an alternative to a tent. Simply put, a bivvy bag is like a long stuff sack big to hold a sleeping bag and sleep mat. Waterproof if made with breathable fabric, a small hoop at the entrance turns it into a mini-tent; the plus of a hoop design is the option of a mozzie screen enabling the occupant to enjoy the view without being bitten. Not to be confused with non-breathable plastic survival bags, a bivvy bag fulfils many of the principles of a tent whilst not actually being one.

Try sleeping in a cheap bright orange plastic survival bag and you will discover how much condensation can accumulate overnight compared with a breathable bivvy bag.

Looking more like a mini-tent, a simple hoop at the bivvy bag opening gives more headroom and allows an insect screen to be added for ventilation on warm nights

Bivvying is an art in itself and allows flexible ultra-lightweight living outdoors albeit without the space and protection offered by a tent. Semi-detached bivvying is the canny use of a natural feature, tarp and bivvy bag for more flexible shelter. Ronald Turnbull's *The Book of the Bivvy*, packed with information and humour, is a cracking exploration of the whys and wherefores of this branch of lightweight camping.

For my own part bivvy bags, combined with a tarp, have proved useful on backpacking, cycling and canoeing jaunts, allowing star gazing without the risk of getting wet from early hours' showers and dew; just pull the hood over your face when needed. They are useful, too, in foreign fields as a barrier to fleas and bugs in basic trekking accommodation: and on cross-country trips as sound shelter waiting for sunrise on mountain summits (definitely an under-rated outdoor activity). Of course, a bivvy is not essential but is an excellent personal windbreak.

Early designs featured drawcord and horizontal zip closure. As manufacturers tried to make getting in and out easier, longer transverse and curved zips were used. The weight crept up and the possibility of leakage increased; performance and comfort co-exist in an uneasy truce. With the sleeping bag rubbing against them, stitched seams need regular re-sealing. Even if a bivvy bag is claimed to be 100 percent breathable, it pays to air off both it and the sleeping bag each morning.

The simple tube style makes a fairly easy DIY project. My own extra-long design, with proofed nylon base and a Gore-Tex upper, has enough room to drag in a rucksack and a huge hood known as the North Stand. It is not ideal but cost a fraction of commercial designs, was fun to make and, as it only gets an outing a few times each year, has been around for many.

Tarps and tarp tents

Offering basic protection from the sun and rain showers, what used to be a simple rectangle of coated nylon with tapes at each corner to help in lashing to trees has become more sophisticated. Modern tarps have clever patterns and high-tech fabrics, cut and sewn to maximise practical shelter whilst shaving weight. Some look like shrunken flysheets with open ends and sides; they are light, often using trek poles for uprights, and take up little space in a rucksack. They can be pitched in odd places and easily adapted to suit changing weather conditions. In mild, stable weather conditions they have their uses but, generally, are no substitute for a good tent.

A tarp tent such as this pyramid style with central pole offers plenty of shelter from rain and sun but less from the wind – and none from biting insects

Simple lightweight tarps can be rigged in many ways; a proper tent is far more practical if insect onslaughts are likely

'Tarp tents' have been developed to fill the gap between tarps and full-blown tents. They look like tents from afar, have loads of internal space but no inner tent or sewn-in groundsheet. Of course, if you have a tent that pitches flysheet first, you already have a tarp tent – just leave the inner at home. Pluses range from less weight to carry to better shelter from the elements than that offered by tarps; minuses include draughty nights and no protection from nasty insects. Using only a flysheet for shelter on a spring cycle-touring trip through the Westcountry was ideal, but would have been a midge-ridden nightmare in Scotland's high summer. As with most outdoor gear, pick what is appropriate, adapting what you have rather than spending a fortune trying to cover every eventuality. I once met a couple of lads touring Ireland by mountain bike. Their 'tent' was a nylon car cover stretched between their bikes: 'We had to use it or not bother coming.' Their bikes were not ideal either, but they were having a grand time.

Care

Forethought when pitching goes a long way to avoiding cleaning, maintenance and repair (see Chapter 3). Clearing away gravel, twigs and other debris – the little bits you find digging into your knees when it is too much bother to re-pitch the tent –reduces the chances of tiny holes appearing in the groundsheet. Using a cheap tarp or durable thin foam underlay under the groundsheet will help protect it and is far easier to clean. Sweeping out the tent takes just a couple of minutes; otherwise, when the tent is tightly packed away, that debris can puncture fabric. Before you know it, that tiny hole has become a tear.

Even synthetic fabrics suffer from mildew, so airing the tent and drying it completely is a care basic. Despite all the ingenious ideas that suppliers come up with, most tents are likely to have condensation inside in the morning. If it hasn't rained the tendency is to pack it away as it appears to be dry, and it's then not looked at for weeks. The next time it is pitched you are likely to encounter strange patches, growths and smells.

A light foam underlay helps to protect a sewn-in groundsheet

Reproofing sections or the whole tent yourself is possible, but you may prefer to send it off to a specialist. It is easy to mistake condensation for rain leakage through fabric or seams; a few moments' investigation and reflection should make it obvious. If you're tempted to clean stains off the tent, avoid detergents or washing up liquid as they will affect the waterproofing. There are proprietary tent cleaners available (see Appendix B).

Checking out guylines, tensioners, eyelets, knots, zips and poles for damage each time the tent is used is a basic element of care rarely done, particularly when packing it away. All the luminous guylines and pegs and bright ribbons tied on cannot beat the laws of physics. Guylines seem to exert a special force on feet; when somebody trips over them it is all too easy for the tent fabric or poles to be damaged. By and large, tents are durable and resilient but over time the various components will wear and suffer damage. Hopefully a small spares and repair kit won't be needed, but it makes sense to keep one handy.

Keeping a simple repair kit handy nips problems in the bud

Zips can take quite a beating so it helps if they run smoothly. They tend to get yanked all ways and can be put under quite a strain so make sure the stitching stays sound; whip out the needle and thread before loose threads lead to frayed tent fabric. If a door or insect screen will not zip up easily, reposition the pegs rather than trying to force the zip.

Making sure that a new tent has all the right bits is easily done in the shop, but always check it over as soon as possible when you get it home. Pitch it in the garden to become proficient at the job, to check that the poles are right and that the inner and flysheet are for the same tent. A mix up with inner and fly was once picked up by a sharp sales assistant in the shop despite my protests that it was bound to be OK. On another occasion the wrong pole for a single hoop design was a pain. As well as enduring the laughter of friends, I found out how hard it can be to break off the unwanted 15cm of a tent pole.

Cutting an old groundsheet to the shape of your tent inner and using it as an extra protection layer against punctures is a lot cheaper than buying a tent 'footprint'. Using one stuff sack for the tent fabric and another for poles and pegs heads off damage and allows for more flexible packing and load sharing. Although a minor consideration, try to avoid shaking shock-corded poles to snap them together as this can cause sharp edges to develop that might tear the fabric. Fold such poles from the centre rather than from one end as this reduces tension on the cord.

We slept in some funny places those first few days: irrigation ditches, village greens, and once beside a public swimming pool, though we didn't realise that as we pitched camp after dark.

On a Bicycle Made For Two
Anna and Howard Green, 1990

TENT NO-NOS

- **Storing your tent damp** Guarantees mould and a horrible smell.
- **Lighting a fire nearby** Sparks could turn it into a colander.
- **Cooking inside** Will either poison you with carbon monoxide or could destroy the tent; most tents are now fire resistant, but that does not mean 'fireproof'.
- **Not clearing your pitch of stones, gravel and twigs** They will ruin your sewn-in groundsheet.
- **Washing your tent in strong detergent** Will seriously affect the waterproof coating.
- **Jamming poles and pegs into the stuff sack with the tent** Will almost certainly eventually catch and tear the tent fabric.

In an ideal world you awake to see dawn breaking over the valley below with the stove ready for the morning brew. High in your eyrie, the tent faces the rising sun and all is well with the world. Would that it were always so. Hard-won lessons mean that forward planning now has a fairly high priority.

On a trip to Corsica to explore the GR20 long-distance path running the length of the island, casual planning had the trip unravelling from the start. Confident that methylated spirits would be readily available, the trusty Trangia had been packed along with a new (empty) fuel bottle to avoid a strip search at the airport. Wandering around Ajaccio's streets at noon, it became apparent that no shops opened until 2pm and, when they did, nobody had 'le meths'. By 4pm the bus to the village at the walk's start had left and it was time to fall back on the universally reliable Camping Gaz (as it was then). Buying a picnic stove and gas cartridges took only minutes, but the day felt wasted.

The first bus in the morning left early – too early to head up the coast to a camp-site. Instead, with a couple of beers and some fresh food, we headed out of town. A pleasant park seemed an ideal place to eat and bivvy, ready for an early start. It almost worked out. As night fell, so the gendarmes arrived and moved us on. Happily, they recognised that we were outdoor folk rather than vagrants but the monument to Napoleon deserved respect (it had escaped our attention).

By now it was dark and we had forgotten our torches in the mad rush to catch a train to the airport. Stumbling along the road, we considered options. The tight budget ruled out a hotel, and the houses lining the road ruled out pitching our little tent. On we strode with fingers crossed, until we noticed a rough track off to our left. It didn't look like the driveway of a house so we peeled off. Before long, level ground opened up and we dropped the packs. Distant thunder meant we decided to pitch the flysheet only, in case of rain, and were soon asleep.

After such a long fraught day, it was a combination of the heat of the sun full on the tent and a horrible smell that woke me in the morning. Unzipping the fly, it became obvious that we were camped on a rubbish tip. Waking my brother, he slipped out of his sleeping bag and trod on a dead rat. It took just minutes to regain the road and head for town. The bus left with us clutching new torches tightly. We agreed that one day we would laugh about the experience. We did – about three years later.

4

SHELTER

SLEEPING

Any successful outdoor venture begins with a warm, dry
sleeping bag. There is no such thing as the perfect sleeping bag.

Song of the Paddle Bill Mason, 1988

In the bag
Comfort is the key to sound sleep. It's about achieving a combination of adjustable warmth and no aches and pains from cold hard ground; a poor night's sleep can cast a pall

over otherwise enjoyable outdoor fun. A sleeping bag is the obvious option for insulation from the cold, and come in a variety of styles, constructions and fills.

For years advice on sleeping bag selection usually began with 'buy the best you can afford', 'best' in this case usually interpreted as 'the warmest'. This seemed too simplistic and, as all the advice on clothing stressed flexible layering, picking only one sleeping bag seemed a tad contradictory. Most of us cannot afford to have a range of sleeping bags to hand to suit a variety of situations. Your budget will help you decide what bag to pick but a full-length zip, an insulating sleep mat and a bag liner will add several degrees of comfort and flexibility. Have a chat with staff in a good outdoor shop. Feel the weight, check the packed size, get inside a variety of bags to check length and width before parting with cash, and make sure that you buy a decent sleep mat as well.

It is easy to be bamboozled by warmth ratings and the technical details of fillings and linings, but the only way to find out what suits you is to experiment. Borrowing sleeping bags makes sense before buying; ask around family and friends. Your own metabolism, what you have eaten, how tired you are, the time of year, altitude, bag design and ground insulation all affect how warm you feel, especially in the early hours of the morning. The question, 'Will this sleeping bag keep me warm?' is just about impossible to answer unless you're considering a polar expedition bag for summer camping in Cornwall. In the UK warmth is usually the key factor to consider, but when camping in hotter countries being cool takes precedence. Sheet sleeping bags can be treated easily with insect repellent; keep a light fleece blanket handy to pull over you as the air temperature drops.

When deciding how warm a bag you need bear in mind the old army saying, 'Travel light, freeze at night'.

There are many factors involved in sleeping bag manufacture: style, shape, fill, materials, design features, stuff sacks. Design details include draught baffles behind no-snag zips, one-handed 'hood' drawcord closure and a variety of ways of holding insulating fill in place. Compromises are inevitable: a full-length zip, for instance, adds weight but offers greater flexibility in temperature control.

Sleeping bags work by trapping a layer of still air warmed by body heat that acts as a barrier to the cold. At home, you lie on a thick mattress in a warm house. When camping both the bedding you lie under and also what you lie on are important. The ground can draw heat from the body, leaving you feeling cold, especially in the colder early hours of the morning. A sleeping mat will help in reducing the loss of body heat through the compression of insulating fill by body weight. However much you roll and wriggle through the night, you will be insulated all round.

Zips allow users to adjust heat retention

This category of gear has seen many developments in the use of recycled fabrics, fills and components. Whether using completely recycled or part-recycled elements, it is now hard to buy a sleeping bag that does not have its eco credentials printed on recycled card. Read the small print and be aware that the headlong rush of a few years ago into totally recycled products has mutated into a more practical assessment of sustainability with the considerations of being fit for purpose, durability and longevity. In due course, claims and counter-claims will settle into an industry-wide standard that is easy to follow.

As consumers have become aware of how down has been harvested, its humane collection has assumed a greater significance in the products on offer.

Temperature ratings

Sleeping bag manufacturers use the European test EN 13537 for temperature ratings more widely these days. Many will also use their own categories such as 'one season' and the like. Most of us have little idea what the temperature will be like at 4am in a tent in, say, Mid Wales in April, so the information is of little use except in comparing bags. It is difficult to be precise, and most ratings assume you will be sleeping clothed and well insulated from the ground.

Despite the existence of European and British standards there is no reliable way of judging whether or not a sleeping bag will be comfortable for an individual other than personal experience. Suppliers and testing bodies are not trying to con consumers with exaggerated claims; there are far too many variables affecting comfort, so comparisons between manufacturers can be difficult to assess with accuracy. It is not just the amount of fill that influences warmth but its ability to loft and the shape and features of the sleeping bag.

As similar bags will be used in all sorts of weather and temperatures with differing amounts of ground insulation by people who may be warm or cold sleepers, in a tent or bivvy bag, well fed or hungry, it makes sense to regard all published warmth or comfort ratings as a rough guide only.

Fills

'Loft' is the ability of the fill of a sleeping bag to expand from its compressed state to form an effective layer of trapped air able to be warmed by body heat for insulation. Whether the fill is natural or synthetic is a key factor in weight, price and performance. In a shop you can get a rough idea of how a bag will loft by taking it out of its stuff sack, rolling it out and 'pumping' it up by opening and closing the neck rapidly; a little experimentation helps. It is also a useful way of accelerating loft when camping.

Most sleeping bags are filled with natural materials such as down, feathers, a mix of both or with synthetic fibres; fleece and fibre pile options are available.

- **Natural** Fluffy down (the under-plumage of ducks and geese) is by far the best natural insulator. It is light, easily compressed (so packs small) and its loft recovers fully when shaken out. Initially costing much more than synthetic fills, down bags will last for years and years if looked after well. The downside is that they are next to useless when wet and difficult to dry on the trail, but the simple answer is to keep your bag dry. With modern outer fabrics, waterproof stuff sacks and quality tents, it really is not difficult to achieve. Down bags can deliver greater warmth, less weight and lower bulk than similar performing synthetic bags, though the gap is narrowing. Down is often mixed with less effective feathers (feel for the stiff quills) to reduce cost so make sure you know what you are looking at. Hopefully, you will know if you are allergic to down.

- **Synthetic** fibres These fills come in a variety of forms and effectiveness. Overall they are cheaper, heavier, bulkier and do not last as long as quality down. However, they maintain insulation when wet and will dry fast. Synthetic fills are made up from layers of fibres, known as 'batts', sewn to fabric to keep them in place. Some of these fibres are hollow, mimicking animal fur by trapping warm air, and helping to account for price differences along with varying construction techniques in apparently identical bags. Others, such as Primaloft, mimic the qualities of down closely and feel very similar.

(left) Down clusters
(below) Primaloft synthetic fill

The liner considerably improves the comfort of this lightweight summer version of the virtually indestructible Buffalo sleeping bag

Fleece may be ideal for use in mild weather or as a sleeping bag liner when the temperature drops; a light fleece blanket is useful as flexible extra insulation in the depths of winter.

- **Buffalo** Using fibre pile and Pertex fabric, the unique shape of the bags in this layered system reflects the unique combination of materials used. The result is superb instant warmth, durability, flexibility and very easy care. A Buffalo Lightweight Outer has been my favourite summer bag for years; it is light, packs down well, and a liner extends its comfort range. It also stays warm when wet, is easy to wash and has a front zip which makes getting in and out really easy. Another plus is the availability of sizes from small to extra large.

Fabrics

The fabric containing the fill should be breathable to allow body moisture vapour to escape rather than condense and spoil the insulation. If you are planning to always sleep in a tent the extra expense of windproof and waterproof fabric for the shell or outer is really unnecessary. For the inner fabric, cotton is soft and comfortable but absorbs moisture whilst taffeta nylon warms quickly, breathes well and feels cosy. Closely woven Pertex synthetic fabric is light, tough, down-proof, highly breathable and water repellent, making it a popular choice for quality down bags.

Design

The combination of effective warmth retention, lower weight and bulk plus cost reduction has seen the convergence of lightweight sleeping bag designs into a 'mummy' shape with a cowl hood that fits snugly around the head and often tapers from hips to feet.

To achieve weight and/or price reductions, manufacturers have dreamt up a variety of ingenious options. These range from different amounts of fill on top and bottom of the bag to sliding a sleeping mat into a sleeve on the underside with no fill.

Ultralight bags may taper sharply, reduce width and dispense with a mummy hood, zip and other design features to achieve even greater weight saving.

As the weight of a bag can be reduced significantly by squeezing the dimensions it is important to try it on for size before buying, not only to ensure it is big enough to sleep in comfortably but also to avoid crushing the loft of the bag and losing insulation. Wriggling around on a shop floor is less uncomfortable than shivering through the night in a tent.

Combination 'systems of down and synthetic filled bags and a thermal liner come and go. Despite offering great flexibility in use, they rarely seem to last long on the market before being withdrawn.

4

Construction

A variety of methods of construction are used in sleeping bag manufacture reflecting type and amount of fill, function and cost. A differential cut – with the inner smaller than the outer shell – ensures that insulation can loft fully

Before buying a sleeping bag do more than feel the fill, get in it and check that it is big enough for comfort.

SHELTER

for maximum warmth. The amount of fill and method of sewing affects the extent of that difference in cut. The simple stitching of sewn-through construction – both synthetic and down – is relatively cheap to make but leaves cold spots where inner and shell are stitched directly together. Curiously, it is used in both cheap synthetic bags and to save weight in ultralight down-filled bags for adventure racing and mountain marathons.

More sophisticated designs for down bags use fabric walls known as 'baffles', and a bigger differential between inner and outer shell to ensure an even distribution of insulation. These baffles (basically box, slant and 'V') at quilt lines avoid cold spots by creating smaller spaces to hold the down fill in place. It is very effective but the most expensive manufacturing method; baffle height and amount of fill affect loft and, thus, warmth. The number, shape and direction of the channels created by baffles reflects the sophistication of design and overall performance. Bags made from fleece and fibre pile need only simple stitching in construction as the insulation is built into the fabric. Whilst less effective than other forms of insulation, they offer robust, cheaper, easy-to-care-for options that are ideal for warm weather use and as sleeping bag liners.

There are several different ways to construct bags using synthetic fills which further helps to account for price differences:

- Single layer – one layer of fill sewn to the outer and lining
- Double offset – twin single layers overlapped to reduce cold spots
- Shingle – no cold spots as overlapping sheets of fibre are sewn to the outer and the lining.

Well-insulated from head to toe in a mummy-shaped design

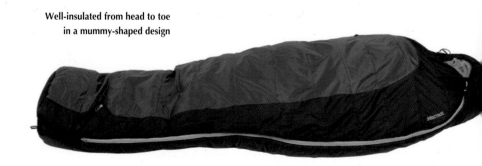

- **Zip** A two-way full-length zip allows flexibility in use with ventilation options (unzip the bag from the foot) and getting in and out easier. They should run smoothly, but take care when zipping up or down not to catch the fabric. If you intend to join two bags together, make sure one has a right-hand zip and the other a left. A full-length zip also offers the possibility of adding a panel to increase the size of a sleeping bag.

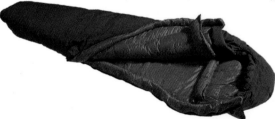

A two-way full-length zip allows flexibility in use with ventilation options (unzip the bag from the foot) and makes getting in and out easier. They should run smoothly but take care not to catch the fabric

- **Hood and collar** As a great deal of body heat can be lost through the head, most sleeping bags have a hood that can be drawn up snugly in cooler weather. Known as a neck or shoulder collar, an insulated tube is sewn in at the base of the hood and aims to stop heat loss; a quick release drawcord will pull it close. Most sleeping bags have an insulated flap or baffle that lies behind the zip to stop body heat seeping out.

A full-length zip offers the possibility of adding a panel to increase the bag size

As a great deal of body heat can be lost through the head, most sleeping bags have a hood that can be drawn up snugly in cooler weather

- **Foot** Whatever the shape (circular, square, rectangular, trapezoid) a box section at the end of the bag helps to maintain a layer of insulation around feet without it being compressed.

A box section at the end of the bag helps to maintain a layer of insulation around feet

4

SHELTER

Cleaning

It is possible to write thousands of words on the cleaning of lightweight sleeping bags, but the best advice is the simplest – follow the manufacturer's instructions. All have comprehensive advice on offer and following it loads the dice in favour of a successful outcome. If something does go wrong, you can go back to the supplier with confidence rather than fudging what you did.

If you decide to wash a down sleeping bag, try to use a big machine at a launderette to minimise the risk of damage, preferably using a cleaner such as Nikwax Down Wash and definitely no detergent or fabric conditioner. Once spun dry well; a long tumble on a low heat in a dryer, with plenty of pauses to break up clumps of fill, should produce a good result. Alternatively, wash it gently by hand in a bath. At first the sodden mess of fabric and fill will seem impossible to restore, but patience and application will result in success. Synthetic fill bags can also be washed fairly easily at home in a washing machine or in the bath with reasonable care. Lift sopping wet bags carefully to avoid tearing stitching.

A sheet liner (see below) will absorb body oils and sweat reducing the need to wash bags and, by keeping them clean, help maintain their efficiency

Storing and care

Between trips, try to avoid dumping everything in a corner of the garage or loft. Unpack, clean up and store properly to ensure your comfort on the next outing. Down or synthetic, the overall advice for sleeping bag storage is more or less the same. As soon as you can, hang up your bags to air off properly over a few days; moisture will dry out and the bag will feel fresher the next time you snuggle in.

Once aired off, store them loose in a large breathable sack. Being jammed for months on end in a stuff sack reduces any material's ability to loft. Many sleeping bags come with a mesh bag but it is quite easy to make your own, or a pillowcase will do the job. Keep the compression stuff sack in the large sack or tied on handily (there is a stuff sack gremlin who is a close relative of the missing sock bandit who lives in most washing machines).

Do
- Stuff your sleeping bag into its bag foot first rather than rolling it up before trying to pack it away – it is much easier and cuts out wear on the same places.
- Pull it out carefully when unpacking rather than tugging hard and risking damage to the stitching.

- Wear socks and a base layer in your bag. As well as extra warmth, they will reduce dirt and sweat damage.
- Use a sheet liner.
- Air off your bag as soon as possible after each use.

Don't
- Use a top-loading washing machine – it may tear your bag apart.
- Use strong soap or detergent.
- Use a small domestic tumble dryer; they are too small, may be too hot and could damage both fabric and filling.
- Lift your bag from just one end when it's wet as the weight of water may rip through stitching.
- Leave it out regularly in strong sun for hours to dry as the UV rays may eventually damage the shell fabric.
- Dry clean synthetic fills as the process damages the insulation.
- Use your bag directly on the ground; dirt and damp will shorten its useful life.

To the uninitiated, getting sleeping bags into their stuff sacks can seem impossible (and after childhoods spent being told to fold clothes properly, it's counter-intuitive). It's a recurring theme when considering lightweight sleeping bags. One huge bag and one small sack seem totally incompatible despite the fact that the former came out of the latter. New bags are usually rolled tightly by a machine to squeeze them into their sacks. By hand, it is next to impossible to do the same unless the stuff sack is generously sized and, anyway, not recommended. By stuffing it in (hence the name), you avoid the potential damage caused by compressing the filling the same way each time and, simply, it's easier. Compression straps help in reducing the bulk of the bag but do turn it into a rather solid brick; slacken them off as soon as you can.

It's easy when you know how and actually do it.

Once filled, the stuff sack's compression straps can reduce the overall size for packing

| Rolled up tightly, the bag should be pulled out as soon as possible after purchase and repacked or hung up in a big storage bag | Hold the bag at the foot with one hand and the mouth of the stuff sack with the other. Throwing the bag over your shoulder helps to avoid picking up dirt and debris on the outer and keeps a degree of control over it | Push the foot right down to the bottom of the stuff sack |

| Carry on feeding the bag into the sack, keeping a tight grip on both and spreading the bag evenly inside. It may seem highly unlikely that it will all fit in – but it will | When almost fully packed the stuffing gets more difficult so holding it between your knees helps with gripping the stuff sack | At the last gasp, you might need to push down really hard before drawing the end closed | When the bag is fully in the sack, pull the drawstring tight with one hand whilst pushing down hard into the sack with the other |

Sleep mats

Once upon a time, the received wisdom was to lay out spare clothing to form a simple (ineffective) mattress and to scoop out a small hole for the hip when lightweight camping. I am sure that my years spent sleeping like that have contributed to the aches and pains in joints that erupt now and then.

Closed-cell foam mats and self-inflating air mats are practical ways of ensuring a comfortable night's sleep, insulated from the cold hard ground and damp. Some foam mats are simple; others have a more sophisticated multi-layer construction for greater insulation and comfort. More comfort is offered by self-inflating mats. Opening a simple valve with a reliable opening/closure screw thread allows the compressed foam core to expand, drawing in air; anti-slip surfaces ensure you don't wake up lying on the groundsheet. As an alternative to full-length versions, shorter lengths protect the torso and hips and shave weight further. Self-inflating sleep mats should be stored with the valves open and the mats flat. If stored rolled up the compression foam will eventually lose its memory and will not expand properly, reducing the essential benefits of warmth and comfort.

Closed-cell foam mats are fairly cheap, simple to use and to look after, being best stored flat, preferably wrapped up to avoid dust build up. Rolling them tight for storage

Self-inflating sleep mats make even rocks bearable overnight

A valve on a typical self-inflating foam mat

will not damage them but trying to get them to lie flat on site is irritating. To achieve the smallest packed size, ensure the foam core is compressed as much as possible before closing the air valve. To clean, a quick wipe down with warm water and drying off is usually all that is needed; if you need to use soap, make sure it's rinsed off completely.

Liners

These are easily washed and dried, reducing the need to wash the bag itself. Further, they add an extra dimension of warmth that can make all the difference on a cold night. They can be found in cotton, synthetics and silk at a variety of prices and styles. Using sleeping bag liners helps to avoid the build-up of sweat and dirt that erodes bag performance over time, and it's much easier to wash and dry a liner than clean a sleeping bag. Manufacturers usually suggest that sleeping bags are rarely, if ever, washed; for most of us that is not feasible, but using a liner defers the evil day.

To achieve the smallest packed size, ensure the foam core is compressed as much as possible before closing the air valve

Pillows

If you feel you need one there are many fleece and inflatable options available. What works best for me is a reversible fleece-lined sleeping bag stuff sack turned inside out and packed loosely with clothing. Some bags have a pocket in which you can slip spare clothing to create a thin pillow.

Some sleeping bag hoods have a pocket which can be packed with spare clothes to form a pillow

An inflatable pillow can double up as a seat on hard ground

We wheeled our bikes out of the railway station in Berwick in the early evening and headed off more or less alongside the River Tweed on the first leg of an exploration of the Scottish Borders. In our panniers we had everything needed for a self-contained trip. Everything, that is, except food for more than a day at a time. With our mobility and the wealth of towns and villages along the way that was not going to be a problem.

The summer's evening was warm. More than just balmy, it was perfect. The roads were empty and the miles flew by as we pedalled, joked and laughed. Stopping at a hotel for a quick beer, we asked about finding somewhere to camp. 'Get yoursel' doon by the river' came the advice from an old boy at the bar. Taking his words as permission, we headed off in the gathering dusk into the first spots of what we hoped was just a shower.

On the riverbank we whipped off the panniers, pegged out guylines for the bikes and slung a large light tarp over both. With some three metres between them, we had created a huge shelter for ourselves and the bikes, pegged down on three sides but open to the front. Unrolling sleeping bags and mats took only a couple of minutes and, as the rain grew heavier, the kettle started steaming for cups of tea. It had been a good day and we were starving, so the first night feast was soon underway with each of us trying to top the other's supply of treats; five courses was the norm. It had been a long day – and longer ones loomed – so there was no incentive to put off turning in.

Experience meant that the pitch was tidied with everything made ready for a simple breakfast and a prompt start in the morning. Both of us like to be up and away rather than spinning out waking and rising, but having the means to hand for a cuppa in bed is a ritual not to be scorned. A quick chat about the next day's route and it was time to seek sanctuary in the bags as the rain beat out an eccentric tune on the tarp. Within minutes, we were both asleep. After a sound sleep, the morning cuppa was enjoyed in bright sunshine.

4

SHELTER

5 HOMEMAKING

Once the basics of tent and sleeping gear have been sorted, it is time to think about other essentials such as food, water and lighting.

KITCHEN

It was pretty plain fare, but although I knew I would have found it extremely unappetizing out in civilization, I was no longer in civilization, and it tasted good.

The Man Who Walked Through Time Colin Fletcher, 1967

Cooking and eating when camping can be much more than just refuelling your body. Any consideration of 'kitchen' involves a number of areas – cooking, foodstuffs, meal preparation, eating and washing up – as well as hours of fun spent planning and discussing menus. Planning meals can avoid disasters, arguments and wasting money. Think about 'easy-to-prepare and cook' meals and plan ahead at home. A repertoire of camping favourites is far better than head scratching on each trip wondering what to have. Camping life is ideally suited to fresh food – salads, fruit, veggies – involving little or no cooking but loads of variety.

For car campers for whom weight and bulk are not critical considerations, gas stoves – using disposable cartridges or refillable bottles – are by far the most popular for convenience, cleanliness and easy operation; two burners extend cooking options. For others, multi-fuel single burner stoves are the norm for flexibility on the move. Even on apparently calm days, a windbreak or stove windshield will help avoid extended cooking times as heat is quickly whisked away by a breeze or burners blown out repeatedly.

To my mind those folk who go down the ultralight route as far as food is concerned are depriving themselves – but having said that, after a hard day's activity most meals will taste great.

Stoves and fuel
The emphasis here is usually on weight, efficiency and cost, but I have always been more concerned about availability of fuel, closely followed by flexibility and reliability. As a result most short trips rely on gas cartridges, with multi-fuel stoves preferred for longer trips. On a backpacking trip

Multi-fuel stoves offer versatility; this Primus Etapower MF can be powered by gas or liquid fuels for small groups

across Iceland there was no opportunity to re-supply and weight was critical so a petrol-powered stove seemed the right choice. On a cycle trip through the Scottish Borders a simple gas cartridge stove was fine for tea breaks and meals. As usual, stove choice results from practical considerations and personal preference. Throw in good or bad experiences and prejudices to complicate the plot.

Stove components can be summarised as fuel tank, fuel feed, burner and pot support, but many and varied are the ways of putting the package together. Stove stability and how much the device is affected by the wind also have to be considered. I once owned a fan-assisted (powered by a battery) Markill Wilderness stove that managed to burn dried cow dung, leaves, twigs and all sorts. It proved difficult to feed with fuel and really had novelty rather than practical value. Under a fierce African sun, I watched a small kettle brought to the boil by lightweight solar reflectors. Fascinating to watch, the process has obvious limitations in the UK.

A single-burner multi-fuel stove: fast, flexible and light

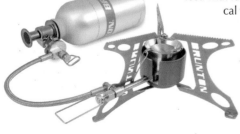

Cutting out some exotic or impractical options, the most usual choice of stoves can be summed up as follows:

Petrol The big plus is that it has a good heat/weight ratio, is not affected by cold, is easily available (filling station negotiations can be interesting) and cheap. On the minus side are the potential danger, messiness and smell.

Yes if:
- You want easily available cheap fuel.
- You want to cook meals quickly.

No if:
- You want to avoid tinkering with stove maintenance and repair issues.
- You cannot stand the smell or mess.
- You want to avoid the risk of singed eyebrows.

Gas These stoves burn clean with easily adjustable heat, from a light simmer to a roaring inferno, but use what can work out as expensive fuel stored in non-refillable metal canisters; sub-zero use may be a problem, though butane/propane gas mixtures claim to solve the problem.

Yes if:
- You want a stove that works simply, efficiently and reliably.

No if:
- You plan to try long sub-zero trips.
- You have to pick up fuel as you backpack.
- You want cheap fuel.

Gas – clean and simple

Methylated spirits Tend to be slow to cook with, heat control awkward and use more fuel than other stoves, but are clean burning without creating a hazard if spilled. Trangia and Optimus options come as complete stove-and-pan sets with built-in wind protection.

Virtually unchanged through decades, the Trangia meths stove guarantees excellent wind protection and has a gas burner option

Yes if:
- Safety is paramount.

No if:
- You want easily adjustable or high heat output.
- You need to find more fuel during your trip.
- You do not want to carry a lot of fuel.

Chemical solid fuel Usually referred to as hexamine cookers, these are simple and light but next to useless for recreational use partly through the difficulty in finding supplies but also because of poor performance, smell and mess.

- Not recommended.

Historically, multi-fuel stove options were not as flexible as they first appeared, often requiring special fuel as an alternative or even different burner options. Life is simpler now and they are an obvious choice.

Stove choice
Through trial and error most of us end up with the stove and fuel that we like. It is really easy to become bogged down with performance figures and (dubious) comparison charts but durability and reliability are key considerations as your stove will need to cope with neglect, accidental abuse and potential damage. Safety and ease of use often go together, but not always. I like to get my hands on a stove

Find a stove and fuel that suits you and focus on food and drink

and imagine what it will be like to operate in a howling gale when I am cold and tired.

On long trips, fuel availability is a key factor. Don't rely on tourist boards and manufacturers telling you, say, that gas cartridges are easily available in obscure parts of Eastern Europe. Consider a multi-fuel stove and a flexible approach to how many stoves you have to choose from at home rather than just one for all seasons and reasons. In the great scheme of life camping stove fuel is not expensive, but if you're on a tight budget both initial price and running costs have to taken into the equation.

Care

Read the advice and information that comes with your stove. If it has an optional maintenance kit, buy it and take it with you on trips.

Whatever your stove and the fuel it uses, the key to long life, reliability and efficiency is keeping it clean. Before packing it away between trips or over the winter give it a final wipe down and store it in a plastic bag. Try to avoid stacking heavy weights on it; stoves are tough but can be broken through carelessness.

Gas stoves require little or no maintenance in themselves, especially those connected to a gas cartridge. What does matter is the hose and pressure regulator used with a gas bottle. Make sure it fits securely on the stove and regulator, and that jubilee clips are in good order and tight. Hoses become weaker with age and may be damaged accidentally. If in doubt, change it before packing away the stove. Similarly, check your camp cooking kit, replacing items as required.

Pressurised petrol and multi-fuel stoves need more attention before stashing them away. (A quick look at a stove's maintenance kit will give you a good idea of what might be a problem.)

- In the course of use you will have cleaned up spills as they happened or, at least, soon after. Now is the time to clean all parts carefully to ensure good fuel efficiency, flame control and to avoid rust or corrosion.
- Usually stoves can simply be wiped down with warm water and washing up liquid, but take some time to clean the burners and dry thoroughly before storing.
- Whether the fuel tank is integral or separate, drain it completely. Fuel left standing can affect fuel lines and cause a build up that reduces flow. If you have nothing in which to store the fuel, burn it off. Pouring it down a drain is no way to dispose of toxic waste. In use, keep fuel clean by pouring it through a screened funnel.

- Oil the pump cup on the stove's plunger with a light oil to help seal the pump against the inside of the compression tube so that it can be pressurised to deliver fuel to the burner. Replace dodgy-looking rubber seals and hose connections.
- Fuel lines, jets and needle valves collect deposits that, sooner or later, will clog your stove. Take care to clean them carefully. A pipe cleaner is a useful accessory to clean and dry awkward places.

MOVEABLE FEASTS

Planning menus is great fun. This overnight meal plan for two has been a great success over the years. The trick is to acquire an efficient light insulated cool bag that doesn't take up a lot of space. This menu takes a little preparation at home, some time to pack and hardly any time to cook and assemble.

Supper
- Snack – nachos and garlic dip (homemade)
- Soup – homemade curried butternut squash (frozen and defrosting in insulated bag while moving)
- Main course – tagliatelle Bolognese (sauce frozen and defrosting slowly in a small insulated bag while moving – reheated and popped back in the box and bag to stay hot whilst boiling pasta; olive oil for pasta in small bottle; small pill box for parmesan cheese)
- Salad – made fresh whilst pasta cooking: tomatoes, cucumber, onion, olives and crumbled feta cheese; dressing in a small plastic bottle
- Flat ciabatta bread – torn into chunks
- Cheese, biscuits and fruit to suit
- Ground coffee for small pot – drunk black (no need to worry about milk going sour)
- Ritter Sport chocolate biscuits
- 0.5 litre red wine in lacquered Sigg bottle

Breakfast
- Bread (sometimes toast) and honey
- Orange juice
- Black tea

Lunch
- Oatcakes
- Cheese
- Fruit
- Black tea – made at breakfast and kept in small insulated flask

Snacks
- Homemade trail mix (see below)

Pots and crocks

Stainless steel, aluminium, titanium and Teflon-coated are among the options in a variety of 'nesting' sets with and without lids. Most sets never quite fit the bill and greater flexibility tends to be based on a blend of items from different sets as well as single purchases. My preference is a stainless steel Mountain Safety Research (MSR) Stowaway Pot that doubles as secure dry food storage with its 'locking' lid, a large non-stick Sigg pan, a Trangia non-stick frypan/lid and an essential pot grab. An old friend, the ubiquitous Trangia kettle, has recently been replaced by an MSR Alpine Teapot – a firm favourite (though it never pours very well).

As camping is a hobby, self-indulgence creeps into the store cupboard of gear with gadgets galore. Some are useful and used occasionally; others have novelty value. Origami-style mugs and plates, mess kits and cutlery sets all play second fiddle to a lightweight medium-sized bowl and a spork (fork and spoon in one) with a Swiss Army picnic knife for chopping and cutting duties.

On top of the basics, there is a growing collection of impulse buys and gifts most of which are rarely used. For instance: anti-scorch pot riser, micro grater, folding spatula, folding grill, small chopping board, coffeepot and filter, stove leveller. Useful (and always used) are a small plastic pot scraper, thin wooden spatula and a simple stove windbreak.

Food storage

The camping larder needs to be wildlife proof but handy to access. Plastic or metal food storage boxes with lids are practical and durable; cardboard boxes and loose food attract unwelcome visitors. A gnawed food packet peppered with mouse droppings is hardly a mouth-watering prospect. Keeping drinks, particularly milk, cool has never really been a problem. If you are on a simple farm site, you could use a bucket full of water kept in the shade with a damp cloth draped over it. Using a power outlet on your car for a cool-box is asking for a flat battery unless you have a split charge system.

Hygiene

Keep your pitch clean, tidy and healthy by cleaning pots, pans, crocks, cutlery, stove and table thoroughly, straight after use. One companion was happy to let his dog lick pots 'clean'; I was definitely not. Clear up rubbish and leftovers and dispose of them appropriately if on the move (do not burn or bury it – 'pack it in, pack it out' is the golden rule) or put it in campsite bins rather than a plastic bag by your

HOMEMAKING

Meals outdoors can be as simple or as complex as you like

We sat down to a special dinner of four courses: pea soup, sliced sausage, sardines and fried potatoes, rice and apple, bread and butter, biscuits and coffee.

Canoeing and Camping Adventures
RC Anderson, 1910

tent. It is one area where being obsessive pays dividends. Keeping pots, pans and crocks clean reduces any risk of stomach upsets; if you use soap for washing up, make sure it is biodegradable.

Cooking up

There is no need to turn lightweight camping into some sort of hybrid survival and punishment exercise. On longer trips, with no possibility of re-supplying along the way, more careful food planning is needed. I have enjoyed a variety of lightweight meal packs from Expedition Foods for filling fuel that is tasty and satisfying without being a back breaker. On the other hand, for an overnight jaunt, a tin of ravioli is quick to prepare. I do like the quality, taste and ease of preparation of Wayfayrer pre-cooked heat-in-the bag meals, but the weight of each means they're not considered for multi-day treks. Supermarket shelves are groaning with gems for campers' larders far beyond noodles and boil-in-the-bag rice; let your imagination have free rein.

If you are backpacking around, say, Cumbria then think about packing supplies securely in a cardboard box and using post restante facilities along your route to save having to carry several days' food at a time and avoid relying on the limited stock of a village shop. Post Offices are disappearing fast but local shops and campsites may help – be creative and persuasive.

A little seasoning can go a long way in cooking, especially with appetites honed by exercise. Salt and pepper are obvious but you can use old 35mm film containers and small cosmetic bottles to carry a range of spices, oils, sauces and dressings for livening up meals without a significant weight penalty.

Snacks certainly help to give energy levels a boost and can lift spirits in poor weather. Rather than the super-sweet taste and short buzz gained from chocolate and sugary mint cake, opt for a combination of homemade trail mix – nuts and raisins – with dried fruits and some fresh fruit such as banana. Dried meat sticks, variously known as jerky or biltong, take a while to chew and stave off the illusion of hunger. I have yet to find a 'sports energy' bar to really enjoy but have found that grain, nut and fruit bars are tasty and do a good enough job on the trail.

Don't forget to maintain your fluid intake. With working harder and sweating more than usual, you can avoid salt deficiency with salt tablets and head off heat exhaustion or worse.

For more ideas for food on the move, see *Moveable Feasts* by Amy-Jane Beer and Roy Halpin (Cicerone 2008)

Dining

This should be the easiest aspect of camping. There are dozens of options in lightweight folding tables and chairs for those going car camping; and if you have ever seen four adults trying to eat a meal off a small table then you will appreciate the value of a larger one. There is also a huge range of unbreakable crockery and tableware on the market, and it is just a matter of budget and personal preference. Otherwise, get as comfortable as possible on the ground, or use rocks as tables and chairs.

CAMP EASY

Anecdotes about cutting down toothbrush handles and so on are amusing, but going lightweight need not mean 'suffering'. For some, being uncomfortable is an essential element of life 'under canvas' or tarp, but a couple of chairs and a small table slung in the back of the car make a big difference when touring by car or setting up a basecamp for a few days' walking or cycling. Stashing them in a backpack, on a bike or kayak would be a physical impossibility. Common sense is the order of the day.

Putting up with discomfort is fine if it is a positive choice, but not if it results from dogma or inexperience. The key to camping more comfortably is breaking down what you do and where you go, as well as when. As most of the items that add to comfort are optional, there is no definitive list of what should or could be taken. Rather, there is a bran tub of gear that can be dipped into as and when – or never.

Anybody who has sat around on the ground for any length of time – cooking, eating, chatting, idling – will be familiar with a growing discomfort in the lower back. At

Any fool can be uncomfortable.

Anon

one end of the spectrum, folding chairs and tables add significantly to the easing of camp life; at the other, sitting on the ground can be endured, even enjoyed, if the weight saved by not adding a degree of comfort contributes to a longer trip outdoors. It is fairly easy to accumulate so many potentially useful lightweight camping gadgets and accessories that the weight is unbearable. Weigh up each item – not just on scales but in your mind before buying (let alone carrying).

Lighting

'Early to bed and early to rise' may cut the mustard for health, wealth and wisdom but cannot be relied on in order to avoid the need for camp lighting. It's not usually a priority when packing camping gear for a trip, though most of us think a torch would be handy. Think again. Tent lighting has many angles – cooking, eating, reading, relaxing, eating, night alarms and excursions (not forgetting pitching your tent in the dark).

As well as where you will use lighting, there is how, and it's unlikely that one light will be enough. A hand-held torch is not much use when you are chopping an onion. You could just cook, eat and get your head down before it gets dark, but that is not always possible. Broadly speaking, lighting needs fall into two main categories:

- **Area** Halos of light that illuminate popping in and out of the tent, cooking, eating, hanging out and helping to avoid tripping over guylines. Everybody benefits from being able to see what is going on, so a lantern for area lighting can be a real boon.
- **Personal** A head torch is the answer, leaving hands free to carry washing up, hold a book and so on. Unless you are planning to go mountain walking, running or climbing by moonlight, there is no need to get bogged down with the technical intricacies of expensive head torches. If the key use for yours is cooking and reading then technical factors such as lighting distance, beam strength and beam pattern are mostly irrelevant – unlike battery life.

Power plays

A light's power source determines how bright it is, how long it lasts, how easy it is to use and how much it costs.

- **Batteries** Convenient, easy to find and pack. Alkaline batteries are pretty cheap and dim slowly, giving you warning that your light source is running out of power.

One of the new breed of
lightweight camping lanterns

Longer lasting than alkaline, lithium batteries are lighter but more expensive and pack in without warning. Rechargeable nickel-cadmium (NiCD) batteries are more expensive initially, but more cost-effective in the long run even though they lose the ability to hold a charge over time; compact solar chargers are an option. Nickel metal hydride (NiMH) are the new type of rechargeable batteries – more environmentally friendly and cheaper than NiCDs.

A typical LED light

- **Liquid fuel** Coleman's lantern is a camping icon and can run on unleaded petrol. As with paraffin-fuelled 'hurricane' lamps, the light is soft but powerful. The hissing sound given out as pressurised liquid fuel lanterns burn adds an extra nostalgic dimension to camp life, and they are easy to refuel. Sadly, for most lightweight camping, they are far too heavy to consider.
- **Gas** Clean, handy and efficient; keep a spare gas cartridge handy to avoid losing light at a critical point; easy ignition systems avoid fumbling and flare ups with lighters and matches. Inside tents be aware that they're easy to knock over, and hanging them up almost guarantees scorching tent fabric (if not much worse).
- **Candle lanterns** I have never found a satisfactory one.
- **LEDs** Many lights these days use these (light emitting diodes). A diode is a basic semiconductor device; LEDs are little light bulbs that fit neatly into an electrical circuit. As they don't have a filament, they won't burn out and they don't get particularly hot. The illumination comes from the movement of electrons in the semiconductor material. Compared with conventional incandescent bulbs, LEDs are very energy efficient, longer lasting, more compact and more durable.

Usually found on key rings, clip-on mini-lights can be easily attached to jackets and bags

HOMEMAKING

TIPS

- Talking to somebody who is looking back with a head torch switched on is a pain – in the eyes.
- Remove the batteries from lights between trips – saves battery life, corrosion, expense and the frustration of no power and no light on site.
- Dispose of spent batteries properly – there is no excuse for just chucking them in the general rubbish; find a recycling point.

All sorts

Camping falls clearly into the category of recreation. So it's sometimes fun to have, packed in your gear, useful gadgets (and even those that weigh little but prove not to have any really practical purpose). In the latter case, there can few

Dry bags offer
total protection
from the wet

Water carrying – simple is often
the best choice

less necessary items than a Backpackers' Washing Line; most of us call it string. However, items that fall under the headings of navigation and safety, including survival bag and first aid kit, can hardly be considered as optional. Comfort and fun are rather different. Because it is fun, there is no irony for me in buying an ultralight titanium spork.

You could fill a dustbin with gear promoted as being great lightweight camping accessories. A dustbin might be the best place for much of it but, if you want it, nobody has the right to stop you carrying it. To try to make some sense of the range of items on offer, it is useful to consider key areas such as carrying, storage, water and general health. as well as some personal preferences.

• Even if your rucksack or panniers have welded seams, a canoe-style dry bag will absolutely ensure total protection from the elements for any gear stowed away inside, even if you fall in a stream.

• Water-carrying options are many and varied, ranging from ingenious hydration reservoirs and drinking tubes to simple water bottles; simple is often the best choice. Whatever option you prefer, it's unlikely that you will always be able to refuel, as it were, with potable water. Having had one draining experience after drinking polluted water, treating stream and spring water has become second nature unless somebody reliable with local knowledge has assured me that the water is safe to drink. The various water purification systems I have tried have all been rather bulky, unwieldy or irritating to use, especially as their use has been in a recreational rather than survival context. Although it is not cheap at around £120, the simple, easy-to-use hand-held SteriPEN Journey water purifier uses UV technology to destroy the DNA of 99.9 percent of unwholesome bacteria, looks like a chunky pen and weighs just 139gm with batteries.

- The importance of skin protection from the sun is vital, and lack of an effective insect repellent can ruin a trip. SkitoStop sun screen with insect repellent provides SPF20 protection against UVA and UVB rays combined with DEET-free insect repellent, effective for several hours (from personal experience in South Africa).
- Not an obvious health item – and more usually thought of in terms of comfort – a chair converter turns a self-inflating mattress into a sort of chair. Very comfortable, the lower back support offered in camp certainly eases current – and helps to avoid longer-term – problems.
- Customising a rucksack need not mean stitching, cutting and adapting. The addition of removable straps, cases and holders can help to make being on the move less of a stop-start process, avoiding the need to swing off your rucksack to access the contents. Insulated water-bottle holders, hard-shell cases for reading glasses and clip-on hand loops for shoulder straps are all easy ways to maximise comfort and convenience. Storage pouches slipped over the rucksack hip belt are great for stashing items such as a camera, snacks, sunscreen, compass, cell phone, binoculars, notebook and pen.
- Storage of a different kind comes with a little screw-thread closure capsule. Mine doubles as a zip pull on a rucksack internal storage pocket and is ideal for information such as name, address, next-of-kin, blood group, doctor and any medication needed, as well as a few bank notes.

Chair converters turn a self-inflating mattress into a surprisingly comfortable seat

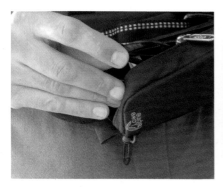

A hard shell protective case for reading glasses can save a lot of grief and expense

Screw-thread closure capsules are ideal for storing information such as name, address, next-of-kin and blood group

- On the health and hygiene front are obvious washing and dental care items. Not so obvious are the desirability of using biodegradable soap and the need to carry a small trowel to bury your waste. Rubbish must be carried out.
- Most of us will take some form of device – camera, cellphone – to record images of our trips. If you're really into photography you'll know all about protecting your investment with appropriately padded and readily accessible cases. If you just like to take the odd picture, consider a padded case clipped conveniently to be readily available. Packed away in the rucksack for safety it's only likely to see the light of day in the evening, somewhat limiting the trip record.

ESSENTIALS – A PERSONAL CHOICE

- **Crocs** These featherweight 'clogs' are outstanding. Lounging about, crossing streams, giving feet a break – there is apparently no limit to the versatility of these hardwearing gems. Personalising them certainly falls into the realm of fun.

- **Head torch** An accessory for cooking, reading and tent nightlife generally, a good head torch should also be considered a safety item.

- **Knife** My favourite Swiss Army picnic knife sits comfortably in the hand, has a locking blade ideal for cutting up apples and spreading pâté, beer and wine bottle openers, tin opener and toothpick.

Light and flexible spare footwear is ideal for use in camp

- **Spork** Sometimes plastic, at others titanium, these combo spoon-and-fork designs beat traditional cutlery hands down. For serious cutting the Swiss Army knife comes into play.

- **Kettle** The iconic Trangia kettle once reigned supreme but, as family and friends latched on to my affection for it, other kettles/teapots appeared as presents. Alternating them jogs memories of past trips (and the tea helps inspire new plans).

- **Buff** A most versatile item of clothing, highly recommended. Ostensibly a simple neck warmer tube, it can be worn in so many ways as to defy description; the original is by far the best.

- **Sportsman's Blanket** Not to be confused with those foil wraps handed out at the end of running events, this is another versatile piece of kit that has many

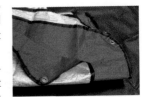

Strong, durable and versatile, Sportsman's Blankets can be hard to find in shops but have a wide variety of uses, from shelter to groundsheet

Easy to fill and use, a portable shower is economic in its water usage and makes a great difference to morale after a hard day

uses from groundsheet to shelter (with cords tied through the strong grommets). I've had three or four of them over the years: not because they wore out or were damaged, but because friends begged me to part with them. Popular in North America, finding one can be rather hit or miss in the UK so when I occasionally see one, I buy it – and suggest you do the same.

- **Shower** Looking after yourself properly is about more than navigation and food, and there is no need to let standards of hygiene drop on a camping jaunt. A few minutes under a portable shower bag can be wonderfully refreshing; the water will warm up nicely if left hanging in the sun.

A note on first aid

There are many first aid kits on the market, often targeted at specific groups of users and neatly packaged. Hopefully, the comprehensive contents will never be used, but that does not mean there is no need to carry them. On balance, though, too many people rely on a kit rather than knowledge to help them in emergencies. Far better to learn some first aid techniques and know how to use what is to hand. Over time my first aid kit has been reduced to treatment for cuts, burns, blisters and stings,

Make up a first aid kit that meets everyday needs

packed in a waterproof pouch. It takes up little space and is used regularly. There is no chance of being bitten by a rattlesnake in the Lake District and any number of ways that slings and bandages can be improvised, and the weight saved is appreciated.

PICKING A HEAD TORCH

They are practical, versatile and a camping essential. The key to their popularity is hands-free lighting; the light beam goes where you are looking and your hands can hold a book, stir a pot or nurse a cup of tea. Lightweight, comfortable and with a wide range of options in terms of beam width, strength, focus and battery life, you'll soon find yours indispensable – at home as well as in and around your tent.

The world of head torches is not as technical as, say, that of mobile phones, but to understand some manufacturers' information you'd need a degree in physics. For such an apparently simple item, there are many design elements. If you are planning to go winter hill walking or climbing, then the detail really matters; if you just want to read in bed without disturbing your partner, it is less significant.

At just 28gm this is a true lightweight combination head torch/lantern

- **Bulb** Traditional incandescent vacuum bulbs have been used for many years for their brightness but turn much of their energy into heat and have a relatively short life. With no filament or glass to break, LEDs' energy isn't wasted in heat and they seem to last forever and thrive on abuse; S-LEDs equal the brightness of many incandescent bulbs. The latest vacuum bulbs stay brighter for longer by adding a gas – halogen, krypton or xenon – that inhibits the build-up of problem soot.
- **Lens** Cover over the bulb; clear, diffused or tinted.
- **On/off switch** Often controls a variety of modes from brightness to flashing.
- **Filter** Tinted covers over the lens.
- **Reflector** 'Mirror' that concentrates the beam.
- **Focus option** Enables some models to adjust the focus of the beam from tight and powerful to wide and diffused.
- **Pivot** Angles the direction of the light source.
- **Headband** Straps, usually elasticated, that can be adjusted easily and quickly to fit snugly.
- **Battery pack** Container that holds the batteries behind the bulb or at the back of the headband. Some have a long connection that allows the power source to be tucked away in a pocket or attached to a belt. Some head torches have a charge meter that gives a pretty good idea of how much power is left in the batteries.

INSURANCE

Add up the total value of your camping gear and you might get a surprise. Throw in specialist clothing and other equipment and there could be a hefty bill to replace it all in the event of loss, fire or theft. It might be that an 'all risks' element in house contents' insurance covers you. Taking that for granted could cost you dear in the event of a claim so check if you are covered and consider a specialist policy to cover gear and activity. When my backpack was stolen, the loss adjuster found it hard to believe the cost of items to be replaced under a 'new for old' policy. Shaking his head, he left with a chunky mail order brochure under his arm. Keep all receipts safe.

No matter how confident you are in your abilities and experience, accidents will happen

HOMEMAKING

6 TREADING SOFTLY

> The trouble with leaving nothing but footprints is that they build up over time.

William Kemsley Jr, founder, *Backpacker Magazine*

Lightweight camping offers freedom and with it, of course, comes responsibility. Being considerate – to the landscape, other people and, indeed, the planet itself – is an integral element of enjoying life outdoors and so it should be, without exception. Treading softly, aiming to minimise our impact as much as is feasibly possible, has always been part of most campers' philosophy. In recent years the growing awareness of the fragility of the environment and the damage we wreak, often unwittingly, has resulted in the development of more formal guidelines for good practice when camping.

As a youngster exploring South and West Wales on foot and by bike, formal notions of minimal impact did not exist. All the camping trips would now be described as 'lightweight' (we had only a tiny tent and sleeping bags) and 'wild'. To us lads it was just 'camping'. Disappearing up the cwm at weekends meant getting away from school and parents on overnight adventures that took on the character of expeditions in our minds. We were careful about sanitation but loved fires and could not imagine a tented camp without one. A fire was our only means of cooking,

A simple site with friendly neighbours

but was more important as representing the spirit of escape from home and adult interference. Automatically, we tried to leave no trace of our passing. Not out of conviction but because it seemed natural (plus, of course, Indians or aliens might have been trailing us).

Our gear was basic but, with hindsight, our understanding of how to live in the outdoors was sound and instinctive. We dug small holes to dispose of our human waste, carted away our food rubbish and were careful not to foul streams. Nobody told us (there was no Scout troop in the area); it just seemed right. Sadly, that innocent intelligence of youth is not shared by all.

There has been a recent disturbing trend to describe stopping off site as 'free-camping', conjuring up images of a liberating lifestyle with no charges or responsibility. Raising people's awareness of the need for treading lightly is an ongoing priority and, I fear, in the UK at least, may soon be backed by draconian monitoring and enforcement measures.

Each summer, National Park authorities report damage to fences, stiles and bridges as 'campers' wreck them for firewood. More than vandalism, such actions are carried out by ignorant, alienated people. The same cannot be said about the walking holiday I had the misfortune to endure some years ago. The operator had set up a camp for the summer in a lovely Pyrenean valley that looked idyllic when we arrived and followed the stream up to the tents. In reality it was far from idyllic: we soon discovered that the ground behind every tree had been used as an open-air toilet and scraps of toilet paper clung to bushes. It was disgusting, yet the attitude of the walk leaders was simply, 'We'll be gone soon so it doesn't matter.' It always matters.

Untangling the Gordian knot of sustainability in the production and use of camping gear is far beyond the scope of this book but cannot be allowed to slip by without comment. It seems impossible to gauge the environmental impact of any particular product purchased. Not being an eco-nomist, the complexities of the production process – including fair trade and decent labour conditions, carbon footprints and the impact of raw material mining and harvesting, combined with production processes – seem overwhelming. I do my best to understand the situation and to follow the pace of change. To many people my attempts may appear inadequate, even pathetic; to others, they will appear eccentric.

By and large, my contribution to treading softly overall is to try to follow the arguments, research purchases carefully and aim to leave no trace of my travelling through the landscape – not even footprints. Sustainability when it comes to camping gear is about only buying what is

needed, making it last a long time, repairing as needs be and, eventually, disposing of it appropriately. Durability is a vital consideration and, as well as taking care of gear, means taking care of the landscape, making conscious decisions to ease impact and, often, abandoning plans faced with the prospect of causing damage.

Sometimes wild camping is the only option

WILD CAMPING

With true wilderness next to impossible to find in this country, the term 'wild camping' does not actually mean heading off through unexplored country. A friend once observed that pitching tents away from fee-paying campsites would be more usefully described as 'informal' or 'casual' camping. It will never catch on – 'wild' sounds so adventurous, even romantic. Wild country gets harder to find in Britain each year, but happily it is still possible to locate spots that feel remote and offer privacy. If you have favourite 'secret' pitches, stifle the urge to share the treasure with friends and keep quiet (before long a magazine will be featuring it in a 'Top Ten Secret Spots' feature and the game will be over). It is really easy to get bogged down in the legal situation regarding pitching a tent in England and Wales where, unlike Scotland (see below), there is no right to such access. All land is owned by somebody and it's the norm to seek permission before pitching. Happily, in more remote places, that is rarely possible.

Wilderness begins in the human mind.

Vox Clamantis in Deserto
Edward Abbey, 1989

6

TREADING SOFTLY

Permission to camp sought and
granted at a farmhouse in the
valley below, so there's no risk
of being told to move on

In the Lakes and Wales pitching a small tent on high and
remote ground is unlikely to have an irate landowner on
your case. Care and consideration go a long way to avoiding trouble – as does a little stealth. A tent that blends into
the colours of the landscape will help to ensure that you will
enjoy undisturbed nights. On the other hand, hopping over
a fence to camp in a field next to the Wye might result in a
confrontation. Asking permission to camp at a farm when
you have arrived under your own steam is likely to see a
positive result, especially if you are asking for advice about
where to pitch your modest tent.

Late on a summer's evening in Mid Wales, a farmer
paused on his quad bike to ask me, 'You'll be looking for
somewhere to camp then?' My reply was simple, 'Yes. Can
you help?' An hour later, the tent was pitched, with permission, on a level patch of firm ground well above a stream and
supper underway. That brief exchange has been common-
place over the years. Often there has been nobody to ask so
common sense, consideration and discretion come into play.
Thoughtlessness is unforgivable. Make what you will of people who remove stones from dry stone walls to help hold tent
pegs. The point is not that they should replace them.; they
should not move them at all. Timing is also a factor. Pitching
in the early evening and setting off again early in the morning
loads the dice in favour of a peaceful passage.

Note that lighting a fire virtually guarantees harsh words
these days. Moorland areas, particularly the Peak District

with its tendency to experience drought-like conditions, are often at risk from fire and wild camping is not appropriate regardless of the care and caution exercised (though check out www.dartmoor-npa.gov.uk/wildcamping for access and encouragement). Similarly, in areas of sensitive vegetation, holes for disposing of waste should not be dug. (Rather, should you be there at all?)

Nobody can carry tent pegs to cover all possibilities, but some ground rules itself out. Shelves of rock offer no chance of pegging whilst soft, boggy ground is likely to be susceptible to damage and is best avoided. Ground that is level, sheltered and well drained, where temporarily flattened grass is the only sign of your overnight halt, is ideal.

Many people observe that the key to a good wild campsite is a lovely view from the tent door, but it is not as easy as that. On a practical level, water supply may be a factor, as well as vulnerability to wind. The soundest advice is not to keep on travelling late in the day in the hope of finding the perfect site. It probably does not exist and it is far better to have one that is good enough – flat, level, sheltered – rather than still be searching in the dark for one that is, in some way, ideal. 'Good enough' means comfortable for you and not harmful to the environment.

When you have packed up in the morning, walk off for a few metres before turning and checking that the area looks the same as when you arrived. Moving stones and otherwise changing the site to make it 'better' is not acceptable. Try to think beyond your modest overnight to hundreds, if not thousands, of people noting the pitch and using it. Ere long, the area will be wrecked, even by well-meaning folk.

If you are not stopping on a commercial site, you must be aware of and practise minimal impact camping techniques.

THE SCOTTISH PLAY

The year 2005 saw the implementation of the Land Reform (Scotland) Act 2003 and Scottish Outdoor Access Code. The Act established a statutory right to camp and the Code details responsibilities and current best practice: www.outdooraccess-scotland.com

Minimal impact

Minimising your impact on the outdoor environment takes more than common sense; we all need to learn about good practice and to be rigorous about implementing it even (or especially) when tired, cold and hungry at the end of a tough day. Any active consideration of care involves weaving some strands before even leaving home with those needed on the ground into a strong resilient outlook that becomes second nature.

Small numbers leave fewer traces; meeting up with others in the hills may be sociable but raises the chances of causing inadvertent damage however carefully pitches have been picked. That damage may not be obvious as most land is somebody's workplace. Not disturbing livestock or wildlife, or avoiding a sensitive area, takes exceptional care. Not chasing sheep is a no-brainer; upsetting pregnant ewes by shouting is less obvious.

With freedom comes responsibility and that extends to actively seeking out information on how to behave, what to do and, if possible, where to camp before setting out. Think about not using a popular spot as over-use degrades places over time no matter how carefully individuals operate. Pitching a tent and lying on the ground will damage vegetation. Hacking it about to make a more comfortable bed, to

A waterside pitch can foul water, erode bank edges and scare off wildlife

avoid groundsheet punctures or to divert rainfall run-off is never acceptable. Ground used on successive nights even by one person has no time to recover, so aim to avoid contributing to patches of dead grass.

One of the key areas is the disposal of waste: human and rubbish. In fact, it is easy to focus on this aspect alone without really taking on board wider principles. Carried to its (il)logical conclusion, wild camping would be banned and there would be no damage from such recreational use. In reality, we have to be pro-active in being sensitive and careful in how we move and camp, aiming at all times to be champions of good practice. Otherwise, we will be queuing for permits before enjoying the outdoors.

Taking care of business

Hearing about people who 'poop in plastic and pack it out' is interesting in a theoretical way, but most of us do not follow that approach. A friend had to abandon his first multiday mountain backpack when he discovered that taking care of business in the open air was beyond him (production, not disposal, was his issue). For the rest of us, there is no single course of action to be followed and, as usual, local conditions have to be taken into account. Excrement is the real problem and those people who dismiss the issue by citing the impact of livestock and wildlife on the landscape are missing the dimensions, for instance, of human faeces in affecting water supplies.

In most cases, burial is appropriate as soil bacteria will help to break it down; using biodegradable toilet paper avoids any risk of fire from burning. Where vegetation is fragile, avoid digging a hole. If a small hole is not feasible, then spread out the excrement thinly to speed the process of breakdown by air circulation (but only somewhere very discreet). Either way, steer clear of water – streams or lakes – and make sure you are at least 50 metres from it. If the ground is boggy, seek out a spot above the water table. The

A simple light trowel makes a big difference in disposing of human waste properly

other obvious course of action for short trips is to exercise a degree of control by using a toilet beforehand and packing out the waste internally. Do not pee in water but out in the open. When buried, tampons and sanitary towels take an astonishing amount of time to rot and may well be dug up by animals. Think ahead for stowage and pack them out.

Don't overlook personal hygiene just because it's more difficult to wash your hands than at home and, generally, keep

clean. 'Dry' handwashing gel that needs no water for effective hygiene can be found easily in pharmacists, outdoor shops and supermarkets. Fouling stream water with soapsuds is not acceptable. Use a pot and pour away the waste water at a distance from fresh water. Using bio-friendly soap is not enough.

Litter

Easy – do not leave any. Empty beer cans and food wrappers hidden in between rocks are an abomination. When you see them, pick them up and strike a blow for decency and the environment. If you see people littering, confront their irresponsible behaviour. Think about high-altitude climbers embracing the wild spaces of remote mountain ranges and desecrating the beauty with tons of rubbish and waste. Think about that selfish indifference to the environment and aim to do the opposite on more modest adventures.

Camp fires

The fire is the altar of the open-air life. Its wandering smokes go upward like men's thoughts; its sparks are like human lives.

The Gentle Art of Tramping
Stephen Graham, 1926

For a variety of reasons (ranging from thoughtful concern for the environment to simple fear) cooking on an open fire when camping has almost become a lost art. If you decide to light a fire, use common sense and follow these simple guidelines to enjoy a fire safely and responsibly:

- Use only fallen dead wood; twigs and small branches may be less likely to be shelter for insects.
- The fire should be contained with a simple ring of rocks which can double up as pot supports.
- Avoid digging it up but try to build the fire on a layer or mound of loose soil which reduces the chances of roots catching fire underground.
- Keep it small rather than building a bonfire.
- Make absolutely sure that the fire is out before you move on and leave no trace of it – scatter the ashes and return mound soil and stones to where you found them.
- Take care to adapt the above when camping by or on a sandy beach. Building a fire below the high-water mark can be unwise if you are not aware of the timing of tides.

Contain fires with a simple ring of rocks

Lighting a fire is quite easy. First, prepare the site as outlined above, preferably in a spot sheltered from the wind. A small pile of dry tinder helps to get a fire going; leaves, dried grass and tiny twigs are useful. Larger twigs, suitable as kindling, should be stacked around in the shape of a tipi, leaving a gap beneath to light the tinder and blow on the starter flames. Lighting from the bottom allows for a chimney effect to develop, drawing flames upwards. Once well lit, add larger pieces of dead wood without crushing the flames. All the advice in the world is no substitute for trial and error. Experimentation is the key to progress and home a good place to start – in the garden or grate, of course.

Simple sites

In the UK it gets harder each year to justify wild camping as the pressure on our fragile environments increases inexorably. Big commercial sites usually hold little appeal but many farm sites offer the best of both worlds – a taste of wild country combined with basic facilities. Pre-booking may not be possible, but a phone call usually gives you an idea about space available.

Owners of such sites generally have a relaxed approach, probably partly due to the fact that many are run as an additional income for the farm but also down to the people who use them. Site offices and shops are rare, and you can usually pitch where you like at modest cost. As a basecamp they are ideal and, with research, may suit long-distance trips and tours; no worries about polluting or eroding landscape (and particularly useful in National Parks).

Farm sites usually offer fairly basic facilities and an easy-going management

At one time finding out about suitable sites usually resulted from potluck and word of mouth. Organisations such as the Backpackers' Club have produced discreet farm-pitch and long-distance-footpath site directories for

It is often easy to find a quiet corner on a simple site

Off site but hardly wild on the island of Barra

decades, but it is Internet forums that have opened up the opportunities for research. By default and design, I rarely camp truly wild in the UK any more; it is hard to justify in the long term and has become uncomfortable to contemplate. Pressure of numbers seems to be the main problem. Recalling old trips and trying to raise awareness of the situation offsets much of the disappointment, but hardly compensates for that wonderful feeling of isolation experienced in remote places. Exporting the wild camping experience to foreign fields is hardly the answer.

Perhaps a partial answer for those people who insist on being stubborn and refuse to give up on wild camping in the UK is faux-wild sites like the backpacking pitches established years ago in Kielder Forest.

FAUX-WILD

It's easy in many parts of the UK to imagine that you're contemplating wilderness from your tent doorway even though there's a man-made track or house not so far away. There's nothing wrong with that feeling but those places are not 'wild', hence fake or 'faux'. Even less wild but more accessible and plenty of fun is a new model of campsite. Encouraged by the demand for private non-regimented pitches sheltered by woodland and allowing real fires, the options for such 'cool' camping on small sites are growing. Hardly wilderness, but light years away from numbered pitches on a large more commercial site. There are plenty of leads at www.coolcamping.co.uk.

The emergence of 'cool camping' has prompted a rash of groomed sites hiding tipis and yurts in woodland glades with fire pits, chopped firewood and a hefty price tag. It is hardly camping as most of us know it, but perhaps lessons could be learned and pitches opened up in wild places where use can be monitored and potential damage contained. Instinctively it is a development to decry, retreating behind slogans of freedom, but it might well happen.

In the meantime, using farm sites as the base for exploration is a personal preference and a file is building on those that are particularly quiet and retain, at least, the illusion of a wild character.

> If the camp is not secret, it is but a troubled resting-place... you must sleep with one eye open, and be up before the day.
>
> *Travels with a Donkey in the Cevennes* RL Stevenson, 1879

UP ON THE DOWNS

A long weekend loomed, and with it the opportunity to stretch the legs on a 'guerrilla' camping trip (nothing to do with pseudo-military activity: the phrase was coined by a nephew to describe bivvying). The South Downs were an unknown quantity but it took no time to pick out the section from Amberley to Butser Hill. This offered a couple of sections of just a few miles – allowing a morning and an afternoon to travel – and a full day's walk of 12 miles plus. Bearing in mind the opportunities to explore sights and sites along the way, it seemed like a neat plan.

An easy train journey deposited us at Amberley railway station. We set off straight away, helped soon after by the clear track even when mist descended and the only sights and sounds were each other and the tread of boots on firm flinty chalk. On towards Bury and Westonbirt Hills with a steady though undemanding climb before the track contoured around and dropped into a little valley – open downs and hidden bottoms galore – before climbing up Bignor Hill. This switchback pattern is typical of this section and adds variety with changing vistas, woodland skirting and traversing, and walking on a broad track, sometimes grassy, sometimes flinty underfoot. Ancient earthworks abound and, on the far side of Bignor, a modern

TREADING SOFTLY

'Roman' signpost with embankment beyond reminds us that we are near the Roman road of Stane Street which linked Chichester and London. The National Trust has a camping barn nearby at Gumber Farm but our bivvy bags enabled us to pick a quiet spot just off the track late in the evening, so it was onwards along broad farm tracks and the woodland edge of Burton Down.

Despite the proximity to centres of population, there had been an airy, empty feel to many sections and, in the woods and bottoms, it seemed there was nobody for miles around. The chalk made for a bit of a pounding underfoot but the firm surface made the walking easy and it was easy to conjure up images of our forebears making the tracks their highways for similar convenience. Late in the evening we stopped just a few paces from the track for a night in the worldwide Hotel Al Fresco. Sliding the self-inflating mats inside the bivvy bags and under the sleeping bags took just a few minutes. As darkness fell, our little gas stove heated a meal and the hedgerow deflected the gentle breeze. Being outdoors as day turns to night means that eyesight adjusts gradually through the growing gloom making torchlight redundant. By the time it was fully dark, we were fast asleep. It works this way in high summer, but not in the early swift transition to pitch dark in winter.

A very early healthy breakfast and several cups of tea set us up for the day, but all the positive thoughts in the world could not dispel the drizzle, mist and gloomy woodland as we rose over Cocking Down. We know, however, that if you get on and walk, one of two things happens. Either you get used to the wet and it does not matter, or the sun comes out; on the other hand, if you decide not to walk, then the sun will burst forth when you are committed to doing something less active and rewarding.

With the sun shining brightly over the broad green valley of Millpond Bottom, it was time for a break and to air off hot feet. The Way skirts Beacon Hill so we were spared the uphill slog and contoured around, skirting the outer earthworks of an Iron Age fort, before entering the broad dry valley of Bramshott Bottom. The obvious route through a notch in earthworks was a red herring as the Way turns sharply westwards up over Hartings Downs with extensive views over the scarp-edge villages below. Another dry bivvy saw the dawn burst into bright sunshine by eight o'clock before we disappeared into the womb of the Queen Elizabeth Country Park. Criss-crossed with trails for walkers, bikers and riders, we expected to see people galore but instead were surprised by the deer that bolted across our track – probably as startled as we were.

Then it was on through the park centre and up Butser Hill before dropping back to the road and bus to the railway station. A two-minute wait for a bus, and our train arriving as we stepped onto the platform, rounded off a satisfying jaunt through downland.

Appendix A
USEFUL CONTACTS

Useful organisations

Backpackers Club www.backpackersclub.co.uk
British Canoe Union www.bcu.org.uk
British Mountaineering Council
www.thebmc.co.uk
Camping and Caravanning Club
www.campingandcaravanningclub.co.uk
Camping Magazine
www.campingmagazine.co.uk
CTC (UK's national cycling organisation)
www.ctc.org.uk
John Muir Trust www.jmt.org
Long Distance Walkers Association
www.ldwa.org.uk
Meteorological Office www.metoffice.com
Mountaineering Council of Scotland
www.mountaineering-scotland.org.uk
National Cycle Network www.sustrans.org.uk
National Parks www.nationalparks.gov.uk
National Trails www.nationaltrail.co.uk
Ordnance Survey www.ordnancesurvey.co.uk
Outdoor Industries Association
www.outdoorindustriesassociation.co.uk

Online campsite directories

Scotland www.scottishcamping.com
UK www.ukcampsite.co.uk

Camping gear retailers

The following lit of retailers sell the whole spectrum of lightweight camping gear. Some are found online, others in the High Street and out of town.

Blacks www.blacks.co.uk
Cotswold Outdoor www.cotswoldoutdoor.com
Ellis Brigham www.ellis-brigham.com
Go Outdoors www.gooutdoors.co.uk
Millets www.millets.co.uk
Nevisport www.nevisport.com
Oswald Bailey www.outdoorgear.co.uk

Snow+Rock www.snowandrock.com
Taunton Leisure www.tauntonleisure.com
Tiso www.tiso.com
UOG www.ultralightoutdoorgear.co.uk
Winwood Outdoor
www.winwood-camping.co.uk
Yeoman's www.yeomansoutdoors.co.uk

Spares, repairs and cleaning

Damage does not necessarily mean that a piece of kit has to be binned. It might be cheaper to repair rather than replace it, or it may be a favourite that you want to keep. Plus, of course, it is better to keep using it or pass it on.

Stoves and lanterns

Base Camp
The Old Bakery
Clifton Road
Littlehampton
West Sussex BN17 5AS
Tel: 01903 723853 2–6pm, Mon–Fri
Email: spares@base-camp.co.uk
Personal callers by appointment only.

Tents

Tentspares.co.uk
Unit 17, Willow Park Industrial Estate
Upton Lane
Stoke Golding
Warwickshire CV13 6EU
Tel: 01455 213887 10am–4pm, Mon–Fri
www.tentspares.co.uk

From tents to rucksacks

AMG
AMG Services
15 Dunivaig Road
Easter Queenslie Industrial Estate
Glasgow G33 4TT

Tel: 0141 773 5482
Email: services@amggroup.co.uk
www.amg-group.co.uk/aftersales

Scottish Mountain Gear Ltd
Unit 19 Fisherrow Industrial Estate
Newhailes Road
Musselburgh
East Lothian EH21 6RU
Tel: 0131 653 1310
www.imagescotland.com/
scottishmountaingear-home

Down-filled sleeping bag repair
Mountaineering Designs
PO Box 20
Grange-Over-Sands
Cumbria LA11 6GD
Tel: 015395 36333
www.mountaineering-designs.co.uk

Down gear cleaning
WE Franklins (Sheffield) Ltd
116–120 Onslow Road
Sheffield S11 7AH
Tel: 0114 268 6161
www.franklinsgroup.co.uk

Fabrics, fills, zips, accessories
Pennine Outdoor
Central Buildings
Main Street
High Bentham
Nr Lancaster LA2 7HE
Tel: 01542 63377
www.pennineoutdoor.co.uk

Point North
Porthdafarch Road
Holyhead
Anglesey LL65 2LP
Tel: 01407 760195
www.pointnorth.co.uk

Specialist camping food suppliers
You may prefer to shop at a local supermarket
but if you're looking for nutritionally well-bal-
anced menus that deliver taste, satisfaction and

energy, the following will be of use. Try out
brands and meals before committing yourself to
a big purchase.

Be-Well Expedition Foods
Unit 20, King Street Industrial Estate
Langtoft
Cambridgeshire PE6 9NF
Tel: 01778 560868
www.bewellexpeditionfoods.com

Expedition Foods
773 Spring Bank West
East Yorkshire HU5 5BA
Tel: 01482 420036
www.expeditionfoods.com

Outdoors Grub Ltd
9a London Road
Bromley
Kent BR1 1BY
Tel: 020 8325 7068
www.outdoorsgrub.co.uk

Reiter Travel Lunch – travellunch.de

Rosker Ltd
13 Quay Lane
Gosport
Hampshire PO12 4LJ
Tel: 023 9252 8711
www.rosker.com

Wayfayrer
Westler Foods
Amotherby
Malton
North Yorkshire YO17 6TQ
Tel (main switchboard): 01653 693971
Tel (product enquiries): 0800 027 6336
www.westlerfoods.com/wayfayrer

AMG Group Ltd
Kelburn Business Park
Port Glasgow PA14 6TD
Tel: 01475 746000
Email: info@amg-outdoor.co.uk
www.amg-group.co.uk

Selected gear manufacturers

Listed below are some lightweight camping gear manufacturers who have helped with information and/or images for this guide; this is not a comprehensive list of suppliers.

Tents and sleeping bags (several also offer rucksacks and cycle luggage)

Blacks www.blacks.co.uk
CAMP www.camp.it
Crux www.crux.uk.com
Easy Camp www.easy-camp.com
Fjallraven www.fjallraven.se
GoLite www.golite.com
Hilleberg www.hilleberg.com
Jack Wolfskin www.jack-wolfskin.com
Littlelife www.littlelife.co.uk
Marmot www.marmot.com
Millet www.millet.fr
Outwell www.outwell.dk
Robens www.robens.de
Snugpak www.snugpak.com
Sprayway www.sprayway.com
Terra Nova www.terra-nova.co.uk
Vango www.vango.co.uk
Vaude www.vaude.co.uk

Sleeping bags and mats

Buffalo www.buffalosystems.co.uk
Deuter www.deutergb.co.uk
Multimat www.multimat.uk.com
PHD Mountain Software www.phdesigns.co.uk

Stoves and cooking

Brunton www.brunton.com
Campingaz www.campingaz.com
Careplus www.careplus.nl
Coleman www.coleman.com
Liard Firebox www.liard-firebox.ch
MSR www.msrgear.com
Primus www.primus.se
Trangia www.vango.co.uk

Rucksacks

Osprey www.ospreypacks.com
Podsacs www.podsacs.com

Heath and hygiene

Careplus www.careplus.nl
Lifesystems www.lifesystems.co.uk
Pocket Shower www.seatosummit.com.au
SteriPEN www.steripen.com

Paddling

Old Town www.oldtowncanoe.com
Perception Kayaks www.perception.co.uk

Cleaning and reproofing

Granger's www.grangers.co.uk
Nikwax www.nikwax.com

Roof racks

HandiRack www.handirack.com

Appendix B
FURTHER READING AND INSPIRATION

Every pitch tells a story
Robert Saunders, 1990

TH Holding may well be the father of lightweight camping but Bob Saunders was the pioneer of the use of lightweight modern fabrics in groundbreaking designs several decades ago. From the transverse ridge Base Camp to the iconic Jetpacker, his ideas have inspired tent designers and imitators worldwide. Once widely available, it is still possible to buy tents from the range online. This long out-of-print booklet is a neat exposition of lightweight tent design. If you see a copy, buy it and brush up your outdoor history.

Contact: Robert Saunders, Five Oaks Lane, Chigwell, Essex, IG7 4QP; tel: 020 8500 2447; www.robertsaunders.co.uk

Ray Jardine's Adventure Page
www.rayjardine.com
Ray Jardine is a fascinating adventurer whose book *Beyond Backpacking* prompted the ultralight outdoor travel revolution of recent years. Eccentric to some and a visionary to many, he is the author of several other titles including *Trail Life*, the updated sequel to *Beyond Backpacking* which builds on '25,000 miles of trail-tested know-how', and *The Ray-Way Tarp Book*. This website is an idiosyncratic treasure trove of information and inspiration – a fascinating insight into the world of this modern-day Renaissance man. The site features lightweight adventures ranging from long-distance backpacking through sea kayaking, canoeing, round-the-world sailing, ocean rowing, bicycle touring, to skiing to the South Pole and mountaineering. Thought provoking and fun, the 'Ray Way' offers an uplifting alternative view on life that challenges conventional thinking about more than gear.

Abbey, Edward. *Desert Solitaire* (Touchstone 1990)

Beer, Amy-Jane and Halpin, Roy. *Moveable Feasts* (Cicerone 2008)

Booth, Derek. *Backpacker's Handbook* (Robert Hale 1972)

Blyton, Enid. *Five Go Off To Camp* (Hodder and Stoughton 1945)

Cox, Jack. *Lightweight Camping* (Lutterworth Press 1972)

Crane, Nicholas. *Clear Waters Rising* (Viking 1996)

Davies, Tom. *Merlin the Magician and the Pacific Coast Highway* (New English Library 1982)

Fletcher, Colin. *The Secret Worlds of Colin Fletcher* (Vintage Books 1990)

Hillaby, John. *Journey Through Europe* (Constable 1972)

Lamb, Dana. *Enchanted Vagabonds* (Hamish Hamilton 1938; Long Riders' Guild 2001)

McGuffin, Gary and Joanie. *Canoeing across Canada* (Diadem 1990)

Scott, Chris. *Adventure Motorcycling Handbook* (Trailblazer Publications 2005)

Stegner, Wallace. *Where the Bluebird Sings to the Lemonade Springs* (Random House 1992)

Styles, Showell. *The Camper's and Tramper's Week-end Book* (Seeley Service 1956)

Townsend, Chris. *The Backpacker's Handbook* (Ragged Mountain Press 3rd ed. 2005)

Turnbull, Ronald. *The Book of the Bivvy* (Cicerone Press 2001)

Velthuizen-de Vries, Michelle. *Pedalling Unknown Paths* (The Book Guild 1985)

Waite, John. *Mean Feat* (Oxford Illustrated Press 1985)

Appendix C
BACK TO THE FUTURE

Looking back over the past 100 years or so it's clear that developments in camping gear appear to be cyclical in nature. Following a period of concern about reducing the weight of individual items and kit overall, weights regarded as acceptable start to creep up until the wheel is re-invented and a new wave of lightweight kit emerges. The weight tends to rise as users want more durability and reliability, with almost inevitable increases in fabric and component weights.

Plus, of course, there is the dimension of 'fit for purpose'. A tent weight quoted 'without pegs' is an interesting notion. Without pegs, is it actually a tent or just a pile of material? Common sense dictates that you really want to know the weight of the flysheet, inner and poles, adding pegs to suit terrain, weather and the other usual suspects. Once sold with optional flysheets, tent weights soared when these became obligatory and featured sewn-in groundsheets – until manufacturers addressed the issue and reduced the overall tent weight by using lighter fabrics, particularly in groundsheets. Problems with durability resulted in the emergence of groundsheets for groundsheets, neatly marketed as 'footprints'. More recently, we've seen lightweight tents *without* groundsheets, but with the option to buy one that clipped in. Usually referred to as 'detachable', in reality, these are 'attachable' with an extra price tag. The good thing is the greater flexibility that is emerging.

As further technological advances are made, it's pretty clear that we'll see a wave of durable, reliable, high-performing lightweight camping gear that may be truly revolutionary. Camp cooking is certainly one area that has enjoyed a recent drive for greater fuel efficiency, and the tent world's reliance on petro-chemical derivatives is likely to be an issue in the not-too-distant future. Perhaps the Solar Spark Lighter is more than just a gimmick (www.sundancesolar.com)?

Ethics and impacts

'Ethics' was once a word used in the outdoor trade in the context of climbing. Wider considerations other than those of business and personal lives – rarely came into play. Not anymore. You cannot turn around without being nudged by another company announcing its environmental, production, social, material and employment concerns in its day-to-day operations. Whether stemming from genuine concerns or pragmatic business considerations, the accelerating effect of all the initiatives can only be for the good of all.

Of course, there are many outdoor companies that have been active in environmental matters for many years. It's interesting, though, that so many of them owe their credentials to the drive of an individual – owners not needing to appease shareholders. Overall there has been a disappointing response from big players in the UK to threats to the outdoor environment.

Advertisements promote the outdoors as a lovely playground. The magazines carrying them actively encourage readers to experience the unspoilt air of 'wilderness'. Most pay occasional lip service to the need to protect and preserve fragile landscapes. Sure, editorials will thunder and features promote 'good' outdoor ethics for walkers, backpackers, canoeists, mountain bikers and climbers, but all these efforts are uncoordinated. There's a growing feeling that many of their *ad hoc* measures ring rather hollow. As manufacturers and media get their acts together on the production and presentation of 'eco cred', a yawning gulf remains on making an impact on lightening the load the outdoors carries on behalf of all of us. It's time to look beyond the Countryside Code to promote awareness of sound outdoor environment practices through all activities and across all ages in all communications – as an integral element in the outdoor industry.

Eco standards

There is likely to be much more emphasis on the environmental credentials of outdoor gear suppliers in the future. Two key players in the monitoring stakes are sure to develop a high profile in the market.

- **Organic Certification** The Global Organic Trade Standard (GOTS) was founded to standardise the requirements for classifying a fibre as organic. The Standard assures the consumer of the organic status of textiles. It covers the production, processing, manufacturing, packaging, labelling, exportation, importation and distribution of all natural fibres. In order to be labelled as organic, 95 percent of the fibres must be organic in origin. www.global-standard.org

- **Bluesign** An independent company focused on sustainable manufacturing processes in the textile industry. Bluesign evaluates and rates processes and materials on many levels including responsible resource management, worker safety, water use, air and water pollutants, consumer safety and compliance with all applicable laws and regulations. The most desirable rating is blue, which means that it is the best possible process available, and it is a planet-responsible practice. www.bluesign.com

Appendix D
CAMPING WITH KIDS

Teenagers. Children. Kids. Toddlers. Sprogs. Nippers. Babies... There is no simple way of categorising youngsters when it comes to camping. A baby's travel cot is of no use to an active teenager so be prepared to adapt, borrow and buy as your children grow. The emphasis is not so much about child-specific gear as about integrating children fully into the experience of camping, sharing, learning and having fun.

Of course, there are camping items designed for children and these definitely add to their feeling of being part of the experience rather than just being tolerated – furniture, sleeping bags and, increasingly, tents. But rather than having a fixed idea of how to kit out kids, it is far more useful to have a flexible attitude that keeps them safe, comfortable and happy whilst encouraging a sense of fun and adventure.

THE RIGHT GEAR

Sleeping
For many years parents were advised to tie a belt around an adult's bag to reduce it in size for use by a child, but there are plenty of child-sized bags on the market these days ranging from toddler to young teens. The key for a child to enjoy a sleeping bag is being able to get out of it easily. Having twice had to clean up the mess after a child had felt trapped in an adult-sized bag and thrown up inside, I take easy care bags for children seriously.

Outdoor gear
None of us needs clothing specially designed for camping, but all campers have to be prepared for bad weather. Dressed appropriately youngsters can enjoy

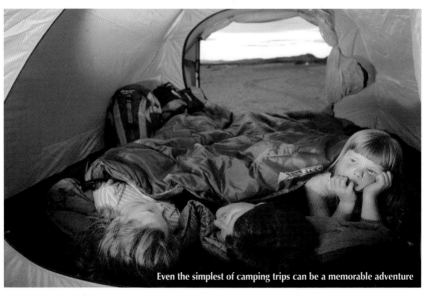
Even the simplest of camping trips can be a memorable adventure

LittleLife's range of travel cots is ideal for camping in or out of the tent

whatever the elements throw at them. The wide range of waterproofs, fleeces, footwear and rucksacks available means that children do not have to be dressed as alpinists to enjoy life outdoors. Even better, the outdoor gear can be used in everyday life, maximising the return on cost. With footwear, think beyond wellies to proper walking boots.

Making it fun
A wander around any good camping shop will reveal a variety of non-essential but fun items designed to catch the attention of children (cartoon figures on water bottles and the like). More important is making sure that children have their own small torch. As well as the practical benefits, having their own light source builds confidence and helps to develop self-reliance. Similarly, allowing children to have their own wash bag and towel helps them take on more responsibility. My father gave me my own camping knife when I was nine years old; sadly, it is now probably a criminal offence to give a simple knife to a youngster. More positively, it is fun and inexpensive to make up a survival outfit, inspired by the likes of Ray Mears and Bear Grylls, with a telescope, compass, signalling mirror and whistle.

Backpacking
There are plenty of rucksacks designed for young teenagers. Most suppliers' ranges will include suitable models with a fair degree of adjustability to cope with growing bodies. None of the other backpacking gear needs to be specially sized for teens and will see them through many years of camping under their own steam. The key factor in backpacking, paddling and pedalling with young children is how much gear the adults can carry.

TIPS

- **Sizing** Do your kids a favour and resist buying outdoor clothing and gear that they will grow into. Pass outgrown clothing onto families with younger children.
- **Cooking** Buying children their own simple camping stove and pans will help to set them up to develop their outdoor skills. Start with old favourites like beans before moving on to three-course meals.
- **Inner tents** Encourage children to come up with their own ideas for customising tents.
- **Toys and games** Essential items of camping gear so make them a priority: favourite cuddly toys help to ward off scary monsters of the imagination and board games to liven up rainy evenings (and electronic games, a fact of modern life).

- **Sleeping bags** Even if it takes ages, encourage youngsters to pack away their own bags. It can be loads of fun but try not to let the tears of frustration flow.
- **Torches** Wind-up versions mean that children can always generate some light and avoid confrontations about wasting batteries.
- **Pop-up tents** These have become more sophisticated, but basic versions make excellent inexpensive play/day tents on site and at home.
- **Extra warmth** When children are cold their whole experience becomes negative so keep a couple of light fleece blankets handy for evening and through the night.
- **Mozzies** Biting insects can ruin a camping trip so stock up with effective child-friendly repellents and use them freely.

Snugpak's Kidi-clips shorten the usable length of a sleeping bag so children don't get lost inside

ONLINE SHOPPING

Online shopping for kiddie campers
www.littleadventureshop.co.uk
www.littlecompleteoutdoors.co.uk
www.littletrekkers.co.uk
www.littlewideworld.co.uk
www.mountainchild.co.uk

Appendix E
BUYING A TENT

As a tent is usually regarded as the core item for lightweight camping, here are a few pointers to consider before buying.

In an ideal world you could nip along to a handy exhibition of all the models that interested you, ready pitched, to explore and dismantle, pack away and erect again. It's not likely to happen. When choosing a tent bear in mind that you can upgrade some elements and maybe embark on a little customising, but you'll not easily add a porch to a design that doesn't have one.

A word about buying second-hand: you might get a bargain (or at least save some cash) but it pays to pitch the tent and go over every element very carefully. Rips are obvious – strained seams are not.

Having decided on an overall style and design, consider the following features and decide what suits your needs:

- Nylon or polyester fabric for durability or lightest weight

- Sewn-in groundsheet: one piece avoids potential seam leakage
- Steep sidewalls to maximise usable internal space
- Tent pole material: aluminium, carbon fibre, fibreglass, for instance; also separate sections or linked by shock-cord? Ideally, all the same length or colour-coded for ease of pitching
- Storage pockets on the inner tent; gear loops to hang a torch
- Zip-closed inner doors with midge-proof mesh doors behind
- Tent colour: a warm glow inside or blending into the landscape?
- Ease of pitching: think what it might be like in a high wind, in the dark or both
- A freestanding design is easy to move about before pegging down to stop it blowing away
- What sort of pegs are supplied? Will they need to be replaced?
- Guyline adjustment: easy or awkward?

Appendix F
DIY TENT REPAIRS

My good friend and partner on many adventures, Ray Wright, is a joiner who believes that ½in of putty will fix most things. With the exception of stuff sacks, however, most home-made lightweight camping gear looks like a dog's dinner and is about as appealing. Despite the fact that tents can stand quite a lot of abuse, it's a fact of life that they will at some time get damaged and will need to be repaired. If you can't or won't send it away to a specialist (and have no faith in putty) you'll have to tackle the task yourself. Every now and then the tent fabric will be torn: as inner tents are not meant to be waterproof they can be stitched up fairly easily, even when torn in a ragged pattern. Waterproof flysheets are different.

The first thing to check is the overall state of the fabric. If the damage is down to material weakened by age, use and the effects of bright sun, a temporary fix might be all that is needed before a new tent is added to the shopping list. No stitch line will be stronger than the material that holds the stitches, and a reinforced area simply means that the problem will recur elsewhere. Good stitches in bad material are pointless. On the other hand, an accidental tear or hole in a new tent with years of life in it demands a different approach. Dealing with damage falls, broadly, into two categories – emergency and long-term. In use, quick-fix running repairs are needed to limit further damage and, maybe, keep the interior dry. Taping and gluing are the easiest to effect on site. However, seam tears need careful patching and reinforcing to be effective over time. Once home, assess the problem and decide how best to deal with

Fabric can be weakened by spills of all sorts so it pays to clean up as soon as possible

it. Some fabric damage can be stitched on a domestic sewing machine; nylon that is cut cleanly is relatively easy to run through a machine or hand-sew.

- **Taping** Every camper should keep a roll of duct tape handy for emergency repairs. Depending on the fabric coating, it may stick well or poorly but should give you some breathing space. If the fabric is under any strain (what tent fabric is not?), then damage is unlikely to be sorted for long by this method. If tent windows are damaged, then tape will do the trick.
- **Gluing** Think twice before applying airbed patches and glue or super glue as they may cause further damage to nylon fabric. If your tent comes with a repair kit, then using the glue supplied

should be fine. Once in place, the application of a rubber-headed mallet should help the two fabrics bond fully. It is a good idea to seek advice from the manufacturer as an apparently sound fix in your living room may prove inadequate in heat, cold, rain, under strain or over time. Make sure the area to be glued is clean and clear of grease and gunge.

- **Sewing** The edges of some rips can be simply sewn together even by hand and then painted on both sides with seam sealant. It pays to add plenty of extra stitching at each end of the rip to ease the inevitable weakness under strain.
- **Patching** Sometimes ragged tears and seams are too awkward to sew simply by hand or machine and it makes sense to add a patch. Make sure it is big enough to cover the rip generously with edges folded under to avoid them unravelling as well as looking neater. Gluing as well as sewing the patch helps to spread the strain on stitches. Sewing patches together on each side of the rip or hole, gluing them and applying seam sealant should ensure a durable flysheet repair. Some people go to extraordinary lengths to find

patches that blend with the fabric to be repaired. Not impossible with new tents, it is a fruitless quest when fabric has faded. Better to make sure that the repair is effective and advertise your DIY dexterity and commitment to recycling sustainable eco-cred.

- **Eyelets** When eyelets fail but the surrounding fabric is fine, any repair usually means having to attach another eyelet (simple plastic and metal versions can be found in outdoor and hardware shops). If the fabric is damaged pick a heavier weight for extra durability, rather than using similar fabric. If the failed eyelet is close to a seam or hem, place the new one further away to reduce the strain.
- **Groundsheets** One night on a dodgy pitch can wreck a sewn-in groundsheet. A tear or hole is easy to patch but dozens of leaking abrasions all over are impossible to repair or re-proof. Consider protecting your investment by using an underlay from the start.
- **Poles** If one has damaged the fabric of the tent it is usually because it is damaged itself. A snapped pole can be sorted temporarily by a sleeve tube or splint and duct tape.

INDEX

LISTING OF CICERONE GUIDES

BRITISH ISLES CHALLENGES, COLLECTIONS AND ACTIVITIES
The End to End Trail
The Mountains of England and Wales
  1 Wales
  2 England
The National Trails
The Relative Hills of Britain
The Ridges of England, Wales and Ireland
The UK Trailwalker's Handbook
Three Peaks, Ten Tors

MOUNTAIN LITERATURE
Unjustifiable Risk?

UK CYCLING
Border Country Cycle Routes
Lands End to John O'Groats Cycle Guide
The Lancashire Cycleway

SCOTLAND
Backpacker's Britain
  Central and Southern Scottish Highlands
  Northern Scotland
Ben Nevis and Glen Coe
North to the Cape
Not the West Highland Way
World Mountain Ranges: Scotland
Scotland's Best Small Mountains
Scotland's Far West
Scotland's Mountain Ridges
Scrambles in Lochaber
The Border Country
The Central Highlands
The Great Glen Way
The Isle of Skye
The Pentland Hills: A Walker's Guide
The Southern Upland Way
The Speyside Way
The West Highland Way
Walking in Scotland's Far North
Walking in the Cairngorms
Walking in the Hebrides
Walking in the Ochils, Campsie Fells and Lomond Hills
Walking in Torridon
Walking Loch Lomond and the Trossachs
Walking on Harris and Lewis
Walking on Jura, Islay and Colonsay
Walking on the Isle of Arran
Walking on the Orkney and Shetland Isles
Walking the Galloway Hills
Walking the Lowther Hills
Walking the Munros
  1 Southern, Central and Western Highlands
  2 Northern Highlands and the Cairngorms

Winter Climbs Ben Nevis and Glen Coe
Winter Climbs in the Cairngorms

NORTHERN ENGLAND TRAILS
A Northern Coast to Coast Walk
Backpacker's Britain Northern England
Hadrian's Wall Path
The Dales Way
The Pennine Way
The Spirit of Hadrian's Wall

NORTH EAST ENGLAND, YORKSHIRE DALES AND PENNINES
Historic Walks in North Yorkshire
South Pennine Walks
The Cleveland Way and the Yorkshire Wolds Way
The North York Moors
The Reivers Way
The Teesdale Way
The Yorkshire Dales Angler's Guide
The Yorkshire Dales
  North and East
  South and West
Walking in County Durham
Walking in Northumberland
Walking in the North Pennines
Walking in the Wolds
Walks in Dales Country
Walks in the Yorkshire Dales
Walks on the North York Moors
  Books 1 and 2

NORTH WEST ENGLAND AND THE ISLE OF MAN
A Walker's Guide to the Lancaster Canal
Historic Walks in Cheshire
Isle of Man Coastal Path
The Isle of Man
The Ribble Way
Walking in Lancashire
Walking in the Forest of Bowland and Pendle
Walking on the West Pennine Moors
Walks in Lancashire Witch Country
Walks in Ribble Country
Walks in Silverdale and Arnside
Walks in the Forest of Bowland

LAKE DISTRICT
Coniston Copper Mines
Great Mountain Days in the Lake District
Lake District Winter Climbs
Lakeland Fellranger
  The Central Fells
  The Mid-Western Fells
  The Near Eastern Fells
  The Southern Fells
Roads and Tracks of the Lake District

Rocky Rambler's Wild Walks
Scrambles in the Lake District North and South
Short Walks in Lakeland
  1 South Lakeland
  2 North Lakeland
  3 West Lakeland
The Cumbria Coastal Way
The Cumbria Way and the Allerdale Ramble
The Lake District Anglers' Guide
Tour of the Lake District

DERBYSHIRE, PEAK DISTRICT AND MIDLANDS
High Peak Walks
The Star Family Walks
Walking in Derbyshire
White Peak Walks
  The Northern Dales
  The Southern Dales

SOUTHERN ENGLAND
A Walker's Guide to the Isle of Wight
London – The definitive walking Guide
The Cotswold Way
The Greater Ridgeway
The Lea Valley Walk
The North Downs Way
The South Downs Way
The South West Coast Path
The Thames Path
Walking in Bedfordshire
Walking in Berkshire
Walking in Buckinghamshire
Walking in Kent
Walking in Sussex
Walking in the Isles of Scilly
Walking in the Thames Valley
Walking on Dartmoor

WALES AND WELSH BORDERS
Backpacker's Britain Wales
Glyndwr's Way
Great Mountain Days in Snowdonia
Hillwalking in Snowdonia
Hillwalking in Wales Vols 1 and 2
Offa's Dyke Path
Ridges of Snowdonia
Scrambles in Snowdonia
The Ascent of Snowdon
The Lleyn Peninsula Coastal Path
The Pembrokeshire Coastal Path
The Shropshire Hills
The Spirit Paths of Wales
Walking in Pembrokeshire
Walking on the Brecon Beacons
Welsh Winter Climbs

For full and up-to-date information
on our ever-expanding list of guides,
visit our website:
www.cicerone.co.uk.

Cicerone's mission is to inform and inspire by providing the best guides to exploring the world

Since its foundation 40 years ago, Cicerone has specialised in publishing guidebooks and has built a reputation for quality and reliability. It now publishes nearly 300 guides to the major destinations for outdoor enthusiasts, including Europe, UK and the rest of the world.

Written by leading and committed specialists, Cicerone guides are recognised as the most authoritative. They are full of information, maps and illustrations so that the user can plan and complete a successful and safe trip or expedition – be it a long face climb, a walk over Lakeland fells, an alpine cycling tour, a Himalayan trek or a ramble in the countryside.

With a thorough introduction to assist planning, clear diagrams, maps and colour photographs to illustrate the terrain and route, and accurate and detailed text, Cicerone guides are designed for ease of use and access to the information.

If the facts on the ground change, or there is any aspect of a guide that you think we can improve, we are always delighted to hear from you.

Cicerone Press
2 Police Square Milnthorpe Cumbria LA7 7PY
Tel: 015395 62069 Fax: 015395 63417
info@cicerone.co.uk www.cicerone.co.uk